CW00456733

'I love this book. Cathy and Mark ha themes in the book of Ephesians in *Up and Alive* has a real depth and Spii understand the whole impact of the good news on the every

Their insightful yet accessible writing brings Paul's letter to the Ephesians to life with brilliant illustration. They break down complex ideas into understandable and applicable concepts that speak to everyone's Christian journey. I would recommend this book to any Christian seeking a deeper understanding and wanting to apply this profound New Testament letter to their lives.'
Revd Cris Rogers, Church of England church planter and Director of Making Disciples

'A terrific book! Inspirational, practical, challenging and thought-provoking, this is a call to engage in our world with a fresh sense of purpose and a deep sense of grace.'
Revd Malcolm Duncan, Lead Pastor at Dundonald Elim Church

Cathy is an author, speaker and broadcaster, who speaks extensively across the UK and beyond for charities, churches, conferences and festivals such as Spring Harvest, where she is part of the planning group. She is also on the board of the Kyria Network, which supports and equips women in leadership. **Mark** is the minister of Fishponds Baptist Church in Bristol. He speaks, mentors and supports leaders in a wide variety of contexts. Mark is also registered blind. Together, Mark and Cathy have two wonderful daughters in their twenties and a much-loved cat!

UP AND ALIVE

Living the life we are made for:
Exploring themes in Ephesians

Cathy and Mark Madavan

First published in Great Britain in 2024

Essential Christian, 14 Horsted Square, Uckfield, TN22 1QG Tel: 01825 746530
Email: info@essentialchristian.org Web: essentialchristian.org
Registered charity number 1126997

SPCK, SPCK Group, Studio 101, The Record Hall, 16–16A Baldwin's Gardens, London,
EC1N 7RJ
www.spckpublishing.co.uk

The authors and publisher have made every effort to ensure that the external
website addresses included in this book are correct and up to date at the time
of going to press. The authors and publisher are not responsible for the content,
quality or continuing accessibility of the sites.

British Library Cataloguing-in-Publication Data
A catalogue record for this book is available from the British Library

Paperback ISBN: 978–0–281–09042–6
Ebook ISBN: ISBN 978–0–281–09043–3
Audio ISBN: ISBN 978–0–281–09044–0

1 3 5 7 9 10 8 6 4 2

Typeset by Fakenham Prepress Solutions, Fakenham, Norfolk, NR21 8NL
First printed in Great Britain by Clays Ltd, Bungay, Suffolk, NR35 1ED
Ebook by Fakenham Prepress Solutions, Fakenham, Norfolk NR21 8NL

Produced on paper from sustainable sources

Contents

Foreword

I met Mark and Cathy Madavan at Spring Harvest Minehead in 2023. I had the privilege of speaking on the last night, where my message of salvation and transformation was also broadcast live into UK prisons. Not having been a regular attendee of Spring Harvest, I didn't really know what to expect.

Mark, Cathy and the team were very welcoming, and for someone who has been involved in church leadership of some sort for over twenty years, I was encouraged by the warm welcome of authentic, relational leadership I encountered. The leadership principle of 'People catch who you are, not what you say' was evident.

Sitting around a table in Minehead's eating hall discussing the evening meeting and what to expect felt like sitting among friends. They laughed and joked, and I realised they were leading out of permission earned, and not based on position or title. Although the subject was serious, it was refreshing that they weren't taking themselves too seriously. They humbly brought their gifts to serve God's greater purpose, knowing that God would do the rest.

I got the sense that Mark and Cathy's lived experience of personal challenges and ministry responsibility – including them serving, for many years, the vision of Spring Harvest – gave them an authentic voice to speak from the book of Ephesians into our lives. I found *Up and Alive* accessible and sensitively challenging. It is a book that informs us of biblical truth and asks the reader: how is this relevant for you and your understanding of Christianity while working out your salvation?

This book has something for everyone. Firstly those who want to 'think it through' and unpack the letter of Ephesians with theological and contextual references, moving from information to revelation to transformation. And also for those who want to start 'working it out' – implementing practically what this would, and could, look like as they apply what they have read to their everyday lives.

Up and Alive moves from information to impartation to application. It's a great practical read, with personal and life anecdotes giving context to the points Paul made to the Church in Ephesus, and explaining how those timeless principles relate to us today. It doesn't shy away from some of the more challenging texts in Ephesians around submission and slavery, and how power and God-given responsibility should be managed.

Mark and Cathy are fully aware of human brokenness and the challenges we face in today's world. They acknowledge those challenges and realities by honestly sharing some of their own, but they always point us back to the One we should look up to. This is a book that will remind us of what we have been *called into* and *called for*. It wakes us up to the grace and mercy of God.

Reading *Up and Alive* will take you through the text of Ephesians, equipping you to 'dress up' – to wear what is spiritually needed for every occasion when living in this world; to 'stand up' for justice and what's right, while living a life worthy of the calling we have received; to 'rise up' with humility and surrender to the One who is worthy and gave everything for us.

I thank Mark and Cathy for writing this book and look forward to the thousands of lives it will impact at Spring Harvest and beyond. Once you have read it, share your thoughts, discuss it with others and gift it to those you feel God is calling to be 'up and alive'.

Dez Brown, Founder and CEO of Spark2Life

Introduction

It is such a privilege for us (Mark and Cathy) to be writing this book together. We both love the Church, the Bible and encouraging others, and we are excited that together with you we will be exploring the theme of being 'up and alive' as followers of Jesus.

So, allow us to start with a question. What does the phrase 'up and alive' conjure in your mind? Are you an early-morning kind of person, perhaps? The sort of individual who leaps from their bed, enthusiastically casting aside their pyjamas and whistling as they accomplish a few dozen tasks before breakfast? Are you 'up and alive' at the crack of dawn, setting off for work more than a few minutes early to beat the rush? Well, perhaps we should begin this book with a confession. We have been married for over thirty years now and one of us has always been more of a morning person, making sandwiches for the children and chatting over breakfast. The other, however, has always reluctantly descended the stairs just in time for the school run, but can never speak a coherent sentence until the first coffee of the day has been administered. Don't judge Cathy, though – she's full of energy in the evenings!

The good news is, this book, *Up and Alive!*, is not a book about being energetic and perky (although if you are, that's great!). Neither is it just for the highly productive or the super-efficient people, zooming through their to-do lists and smashing their targets. It isn't aimed especially at those who have an easy life or a healthy income or those in peak physical condition without any disability or health challenges to deal with. If it was, we wouldn't be the right people to write it! So, this book is definitely not just a self-help manual to encourage you to 'live your best life' according to the metrics and benchmarks of success defined by the world around us.

Not at all.

In fact, we believe it is far more challenging and inspiring than that. *Up and Alive!* has been written for all of us who call ourselves followers of Jesus, whoever and wherever we are, as a reminder of who we are truly called to be. This is an invitation for every one of us to be 'up and alive', whatever our own challenges and limitations, opportunities and strengths, and for us to find our purpose and to grow in confidence, unity and maturity together as a Church – all underpinned by the assurance of who we are, biblically speaking. Learning again how to be 'up and alive' as a Christian community is an important task, because we live in days where many in the Western Church understandably feel that we are on the defensive, on the decline and increasingly on the margins. We need to recapture a vision of who we really are – we are defined, redeemed, called, equipped and empowered by God to live for his glory. We are part of God's unfolding plan, and we are commissioned to share his good news with others. We believe wholeheartedly that God has not brought us this far to only bring us this far!

Of course, living out our faith is not always easy, and many of us, both as individuals and as churches, have been discouraged and frankly exhausted in recent years. The Covid-19 pandemic was an undeniable seismic shift on many levels, and our society is still reeling from the effects. Work patterns have changed. The sense of our own mortality has changed. People's commitment levels and habits have changed. A sense of anxiety and self-protectiveness still lingers, and we know that those of the younger generation were disproportionately affected in both their education and their socialisation. Perhaps our expectations of church have also changed, and now we live in a new hybrid world with many competing demands on our time. For some, their faith has wavered, whereas for others it has become more vital than ever. One thing is for sure – the ecclesiological landscape has shifted, and we are still working out what that will mean in the longer term.

What an appropriate moment, then, for us as disciples (including leaders) to circle back and realign ourselves with the life we have been called to live. What a good time it is for the Church to reframe and refocus where necessary, and for us to keep serving and sharing the love of God in both faithful and innovative ways. These are indeed demanding, fast-moving and uncertain times, with evolving technology, climate issues, increased mental-health challenges, political and economic crises, creaking societal infrastructure and plenty of long-term challenges that remain post-pandemic. So this is a vital time for the Church to be truly 'up and alive'. If ever there was a season when good news was needed amid the bad news and fake news, it is surely now.

Of course, we are not the first generation of followers of Jesus to face challenges. So, in order to explore this big idea of being 'up and alive', we will be spending time in the New Testament book of Ephesians. To be crystal clear: we don't intend this book to be an exhaustive academic tome or an in-depth theological commentary (it definitely won't be!), but we will be diving into some of the themes found in Ephesians and we hope that we will know this letter far better by the end of our time together.

Written by the apostle Paul, Ephesians is a brilliantly concise but comprehensive missive, packed with memorable verses and containing some incredible mind-stretching and heart-enlarging theology. Within its six chapters, we will find plenty of wisdom and insight, and although it may have been written primarily as a circular to Christian believers in and around Ephesus long ago, it is still incredibly relevant to us as we seek to live out our faith and to consistently stand firm in an increasingly secular society.

A bit of background: Ephesus

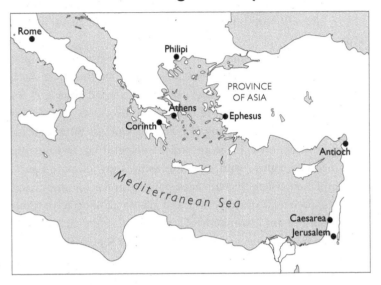

Before we begin to explore some of the themes in Ephesians, including the possible implications for us as we respond to Jesus today, it will be useful for us to consider a little of the context and background of the city of Ephesus, which is situated in modern southwestern Turkey.

We were fortunate enough to visit Ephesus a few years ago. If you have never been to this incredible ancient site, it is a real eye-opener. Even now it is magnificent, with marble streets, enormous buildings, mosaics on the floors and a 24,000-seater amphitheatre cut into the hillside.[1] It's not hard to imagine when you see it now how back in the day, 2,000 years ago, Ephesus was a jewel in the Roman Empire's crown and the capital of the Roman province of Asia. As well as being a major seaport at the time, all the roads in the province led to this harbour city, resulting in a cacophony of cultures, nationalities, languages and people groups living together, with a population of about 250,000 people. It was a city of seriously impressive architecture, including a 21-metre (70-foot) wide colonnade lined with pillars leading to the harbourfront (some still standing, although the harbour was silted up long ago). The giant marble amphitheatre alongside the stadium was used to host performances, debates, gladiator battles and annual games, which were apparently done in style. The city also had a huge library and a market square area, and a city council with government buildings. Ephesus had a thriving banking system, and since we all know that money makes money, it is not surprising that it was a wealthy city, where the rich owned houses with central heating and fountains in their front court-yards (remember this was all without the benefit of electricity!). There were even public (marble) toilets that were plumbed into a sewage system. We sat on those ancient toilets when we visited and can confirm they are as solid as you would expect a stone loo seat to be!

Alongside all this grandeur, Ephesus also held the status of a 'free' city, although it was under Roman control ultimately. This meant it was self-governing, allowed to coin its own money, and had no Roman troops garrisoned in the city, policing the popula-tion. This made Ephesus a refuge and a place of safety for many, including, presumably, those avoiding the Roman authorities.

But situated just beyond this impressive conurbation was something hugely significant, something people would travel and pilgrimage from all over the empire to visit and something so outstanding it was considered one of the Seven Wonders of the Ancient World. This was the temple to the goddess Artemis (or Diana). This temple (or the Artemision) was originally constructed in the sixth century BC. Made entirely of marble, it was the largest building in the Greek world, with measurements of over 50 x 115 metres with 127 columns, each 2 metres in diameter and almost 18 metres or 60 feet high.[2]

One ancient Greek poet from the second century, named Antipater, upon seeing the Artemision for the first time, compared it with the other wonders of the ancient world, saying:

> I have set eyes on the wall of lofty Babylon on which is a road for chariots, and the statue of Zeus by the Alpheus, and the hanging gardens, and the colossus of the Sun, and the huge labour of the high pyramids, and the vast tomb of Mausolus; but when I saw the house of Artemis that mounted to clouds, those other marvels lost their brilliancy, and I said, 'Lo, apart from Olympus, the Sun never looked on aught so grand.'[3]

It sounds like a 5-star TripAdvisor review from Antipater, then! This was indeed an impressive place of devotion to the goddess Artemis (the twin sister of Apollo in Greek mythology), who was the epitome of all things feminine, denoting childbirth, purity and fertility. The cult of Artemis was expressed in mysterious and magical rites, and while the exact meaning of her many 'breasts', or 'eggs', and how many of these rites were indecent or sexual in nature is debated by historians, this temple was a major attraction and a place of worship, with processions, rituals and celebrations aplenty.[4] As a result, beside the normal trade and commerce you would expect in a cosmopolitan port city, Ephesus also had a thriving religious economy making cultic paraphernalia, with visitors bringing and taking away souvenirs of their visit, and silversmiths making their living by selling their wares in and around the temple.[5]

So Ephesus was quite the place. If when we picture an ancient civilisation we imagine folk living a simple, unsophisticated life, devoid of any of the pressures or influences we experience today, we would be mistaken. This was a busy, metropolitan and significant city, with multiple power dynamics and contrasting beliefs all jostling for their place. And this was the context where the apostle Paul turned up and shared the good news of Jesus Christ, first in the synagogue, and later, on his return, in the lecture hall (Acts 19:9). This is where he lived and built relationships and challenged the status quo.

A bit of background: Paul

What courage and determination it must have taken to enter a city like Ephesus to teach about Jesus and challenge the culture of the day. Although we know that Paul was a gifted and persuasive communicator whose life and Pharisaic zeal had been disrupted and transformed by meeting Jesus, it clearly wasn't just clever words or brilliant arguments that convinced so many in Ephesus to believe. God was powerfully present and at work in this great city. We read in Acts 19:11–12: 'God did extraordinary miracles through Paul, so that even handkerchiefs and aprons that had touched him were taken to those who were ill, and their illnesses were cured and the evil spirits left them.'

Paul's ministry in Ephesus was hallmarked by a phenomenal move of God, and the message of Jesus the Messiah's life, death and resurrection spread rapidly throughout the whole region, with significant numbers of people turning their backs on their old ways, destroying idols and publicly burning their expensive sorcery scrolls (Acts 19:19). The impact was significant enough for the economy of the entire city to be affected, with the silversmith traders' protests leading to the city rising in uproar against Paul and his message of Jesus (Acts 19:23ff.). Almost unbelievably, this unrelenting missionary wanted to appear in front of the rioting crowd, but the disciples and some friendly officials begged and convinced him not to do it (Acts 19:30–31). What a place for a fledgling church plant to begin! But it did, and God empowered and propelled the Christian community in the region forwards as the message spread.

Years later (around AD 60), Paul, who was almost certainly in captivity in Rome at this point, wrote a letter to those Ephesian converts, which was also quite probably circulated to other believers in the area.[6] It has been said that Ephesians is a letter unlike many other Pauline letters, which often addressed specific issues that a particular church was struggling with. Nevertheless, the letter to the Ephesians is closely linked to the letter to the Colossians – indeed, of 1,570 words in Colossians, 34% reappear in Ephesians and 26.5% of the 2,411 words in Ephesians are paralleled in Colossians. There are clear similarities in style and content (as well as differences), and although commentators debate over which was written first and why this interdependence is so significant, the overarching themes and concepts are clearly significant to Paul.[7] In fact, theologian N. T. Wright suggests that reading Ephesians is a bit like taking a trip on the London Eye, in that just as this giant wheel gives a person the opportunity to rise and survey the breathtaking landscape of the city, so this letter offers us 'a bird's-eye view of one theme after another within early Christian reflection'.[8] This succinct but panoramic letter effectively brings together Paul's writing and the themes he explores elsewhere as he seeks to encourage, strengthen and teach the believers about how to remain faithful to Jesus and united in his love.

This big-picture perspective of God's love and redemption must have greatly encouraged those first readers. Their past encounters with God may have been extraordinary, but they needed to continue to rise up and live the life they were made for and called to. Yes, they had witnessed God moving in power before, but God was still with them and for them, and Paul writes to spur them on in their faith. Perhaps, like the Ephesians, we too need to retain that big-picture perspective and be encouraged that God is still with us and for us.

A soul recalibration

Last week we took our car to the garage for a remortgage – sorry, an MOT and service! Why are cars so expensive to look after? But once the oil had been changed, the wheels realigned, the brake pads sorted and the gadgets reprogrammed so they stopped beeping randomly at us, we really noticed the difference. The car had clearly not been operating at peak performance because it needed some attention. Some things had been neglected, and possibly (just possibly) it hadn't always been driven with the maximum care and attention.

Now, we will all come to this book in different circumstances, but it seems plausible that most of us will need a bit of a soul recalibration or a spiritual MOT from time to time. Quite honestly, we don't always navigate life with maximum care, or maybe we have just had to navigate some very tricky terrain that has taken its toll. Maybe some areas of our faith have taken a battering in the busyness, or perhaps the warning lights have been flashing in our relationships or our attitudes but we haven't wanted to count the cost or to pay attention as needed. So, we've chugged along, but not as smoothly as we could.

Might we also suggest that Paul would be a bit bothered by the state of the Church in places today? Could we corporately do with a bit of a tune-up, do you think? Might it be that the unity and holiness, hallmarked by grace and peace, which Paul contends for so powerfully, are not always quite firing on all cylinders? As we witness yet another scandal, a church split, a social media dispute or the gentle ecclesiastical slide into consumerism or apathy, maybe it's time to recalibrate and realign with Jesus' teaching again. Certainly, Paul seems to think this is crucial, as almost every paragraph in the letter brings us back to Jesus Christ the Messiah – the only one who can ultimately redeem and 'recalibrate' us to become more like him.

So, to dig into the rich content of this letter, we won't be going through it verse by verse, although that is not an ineffective or fruitless pursuit, and there are excellent books that would serve you well in this regard.[9] Instead we will think more about the themes that arise and we will consider therefore how we might live and respond in our everyday lives and situations. But be assured at this stage, Paul's words will encourage and challenge us to know and receive God's love, grace and mercy, and to live a holy life in the light of that revelation. Both who we are and how we live matter. Our position in Christ and our mission for Christ are inextricably linked. We are called to *be* different and distinctive and to *make* a distinctive difference – because of Jesus.

As one esteemed church leader and thinker, John Stott, once said of Ephesians, 'The letter to the Ephesians is a marvellously concise, yet comprehensive summary of the Christian good news and its implications. Nobody can read it without being moved to wonder and worship, and challenged to consistency of life.'[10]

The motivation for Paul's writing seems clear – that we would wholeheartedly know the good news of Jesus and his calling, and then we would live accordingly in the light of what we have already received; that we would more fully become the people we already are in Christ; that we would truly embody the truth we have already accepted; that we would live fully in the power of God already given to us. Ephesians 4:1 seems to summarise so much of this letter, where Paul says, 'As a prisoner for the Lord, then, I urge you to live a life worthy of the calling you have received.'

That is it, in a nutshell. We are being challenged to live our lives in such a way that we represent the calling we have already received. It is not a calling we need to strive for or to go and find somewhere new. We have already received it in Christ, and now we need to learn to live a life that is worthy of it.

Where are we heading?

Look up

To begin with, we will need to step back and look up. Whatever our perspective of who God is, however large the challenges we face, whatever dreams we might dream, we need to look up and rediscover just how big God is. Do you need a vision check, so you see God and your life more clearly? Let's start here.

Wake up

It is possible to live each day without consciously thinking about who we are or how we are doing. Perhaps we even hit the metaphorical snooze button on our faith when things get particularly hard. But there's a better way, and it involves waking up to the full reality and possibility of who we are in Christ. God's grace doesn't just tweak who we are; it transforms us, from the inside out, to demonstrate his goodness to a sleeping world.

Dress up

Let's get practical: the brilliant imagery in Ephesians concerning what we wear will help us to consider what holy and prayerful living looks like. You might need to take some things off, but you are definitely called to put some things on. Prepare to get changed!

Stand up

Paul isn't one for sitting around and we too might need to exit our comfort zone from time to time. But this isn't about being fierce or militant. Standing firm the Jesus way is very different from just standing up for our rights. So we will learn how to stand humbly but confidently together.

Rise up

Nobody can read Ephesians carefully and emerge with a gospel that is individualistic, and neither is it a casual calling. Ephesians paints a clear picture of a Church called to rise and radiate God's holy life of peace, grace, unity, reconciliation and righteousness. It is costly living, but it is adventurous and glorious living, because we are alive in Christ.

These are profoundly important themes, then, and it feels, at least to us, as though this is a timely revisit to Paul's teaching in the letter of Ephesians. So, whether you are returning to Paul's words for the umpteenth occasion or discovering them for the very first time, we pray the Holy Spirit will challenge, inspire and call you deeper into a walk with Jesus as you read on. None of us want to settle for half-hearted living, and we certainly don't want to miss the potential of knowing more of God's presence each day. Like many of you, we long for God to move powerfully again in our churches and communities, as we continue to share the glorious grace he has poured out on us (Ephesians 1:6).

So, as we embark on this journey together, let's pray that we will be, both as individuals and as churches, 'up and alive' and ready to live the life we were made for.

1

Look up

You have received every spiritual blessing

Have you ever been to see a musical, be that in London's West End, at a local theatre or even a school production? We love going to see a show, whether it is a professional production or a local affair. There is always something exciting about arriving and finding our seats, anticipating the moment when the music begins and the curtain rises. And often, especially in the older style of musicals (or particularly in an opera), the whole experience begins with a kind of orchestral teaser, more properly named 'the overture'. These few minutes of music cleverly introduce the audience to some of the grand themes and major motifs they will hear later as the production unfolds. In essence, right at the beginning, the orchestra presents you with a little melody from here and a few bars of an anthem from there, treating you to the edited highlights of the score ahead – so that you are left in no doubt that what is to come is worth waiting (and paying!) for.

While all metaphors are limited, the beginning of the letter to the Ephesians is something akin to a theological overture, if you will. Right at the start, after Paul sends a warm welcome and extends grace and peace, he then pulls back the curtain and launches into an extraordinary prelude to what is to come later. In just a few verses, Paul, a theological maestro, reveals the condensed, distilled and edited highlights of some key themes and motifs that lie ahead in his writing, as he explores who God is, who we are in Christ, and the difference that should make to our lives as Christians following Jesus together.

So, let's read Ephesians 1:3–14, Paul's prelude of praise to God's glory, which paints a stunning big-picture perspective at the start of his letter.

Praise be to the God and Father of our Lord Jesus Christ, who has blessed us in the heavenly realms with every spiritual blessing in Christ. For he chose us in him before the creation of the world to be holy and blameless in his sight. In love he predestined us for adoption to sonship through Jesus Christ, in accordance with his pleasure and will – to the praise of his glorious grace, which he has freely given us in the One he loves. In him we have redemption through his blood, the forgiveness of sins, in accordance with the riches of God's grace that he lavished on us. With all wisdom and understanding, he made known to us the mystery of his will according to his good pleasure, which he purposed in Christ, to be put into effect when the times reach their fulfilment – to bring unity to all things in heaven and on earth under Christ.

In him we were also chosen, having been predestined according to the plan of him who works out everything in conformity with the purpose of his will, in order that we, who were the first to put our hope in Christ, might be for the praise of his glory. And you also were included in Christ when you heard the message of truth, the gospel of your salvation. When you believed, you were marked in him with a seal, the promised Holy Spirit, who is a deposit guaranteeing our inheritance until the redemption of those who are God's possession – to the praise of his glory.

This inspiring overture has it all, doesn't it? It weaves together who God is, the past, the present, the future, our adoption, our redemption, God's glorious and lavish grace, his redemptive purposes, his will, our hope and promise and his eternal plans. Indeed, in a few sentences we are reminded that God has 'blessed us in the heavenly realms with every spiritual blessing in Christ' (v. 3).

In the original Greek text, these twelve verses are written as one incredibly complex sentence, without any punctuation. It is as if these cascading words seem to tumble from Paul's pen without time to pause for commas or full stops. What would your English teacher at school have said about that? But this sentence, which is unparalleled in length in the New Testament,[1] is less like a textbook and more like a lyrical song of worship, an outburst of blessing or a heartfelt doxology expressing praise to our God.

If we are honest, the intensity or complexity of this passage, and the way Paul covers so much ground in such a condensed way, might leave us a little confused or even overwhelmed. Perhaps, facing such a complicated passage of Scripture, we can be tempted to do one of two things. We can nod sagely and skip over it (we've all been there), or we can try to be that sage who dissects each word and phrase in order to extract every divine morsel of revelation contained within.

But neither skipping over nor getting buried under this passage will serve us well. Because, in essence, Paul wants his readers to start by thinking about how awesome God is, and how extravagant his blessings are. He begins his letter, therefore, by looking up at the greatness and the goodness of God, and he points unequivocally to everything God has given us in Christ. Paul seeks to urgently and passionately remind his readers (and now us) that we should have a full, widescreen, multicolour, panoramic, vibrant and kaleidoscopic view of who God is and how lavish and complete his love is. After all, God is so much bigger and more wonderful than we often remember or than we could ever fully comprehend.

So, today (and every day) we need to keep looking up. Again and again, as disciples, we should lift our eyes in worship, to reflect on and wonder at who God is and what he has done for us. Maybe if we look up for long enough, we too will breathlessly pour out our unpunctuated praise to God for his extraordinary and unconditional love and grace. We could never fully express how indescribably good God is. Nevertheless, he is worthy of our feeble but heartfelt attempts to honour and worship him for who he is.

A hope-filled perspective

Reading Ephesians again will undoubtedly help us to regain a big-picture perspective of our faith and will enable us to recalibrate how we see God and the world around us. It's fair to say this tweak in our perspective is often needed, because as we look up and step back, we regain our vision and see things differently as a result.

As a child, I (Cathy) was captivated by Lewis Carroll's famous but rather fantastical book *Alice's Adventures in Wonderland*. In this topsy-turvy world that gets 'curiouser and curiouser' as every page turns, Alice (having followed a rabbit down a hole, naturally) grows smaller or larger by drinking potions and eating cakes. I have to say, in the name of research, I've eaten plenty of cakes over the years, but I have stayed stubbornly short! In the story, however, Alice always struggles to be the size she seeks to be and faces all kinds of challenges when she is either too small or too large.

As an adult, although I now realise how bizarre Alice's story is, I still think she has something to teach us. It is perfectly possible for our perspective to fluctuate. I know there are days when I feel small (metaphorically) or too insignificant to really matter to God – surely the Creator of the universe might have other, more pressing, things to attend to than me and my desires, dreams or doubts. There are also days when I feel as if I have reduced capacity or that I am ineffective compared to others whose lives seem so much bigger, better and brighter than my own. On a really bad or low day, I might feel 'shut up like a telescope', as Alice described it, withdrawn or overlooked by God or others in some way. There are other times when the things I am carrying seem simply too large to handle. When I look at my own challenges, or glimpse the myriad of financial, political or economic issues, or consider the pressure points in my family, community or church, it all feels overwhelmingly huge. There are so many heavy and complex conundrums I would love to shrink down to a more manageable size.

But this is why it is important to step back and look up. All of us have a perspective problem sometimes, where we see ourselves, others or God in an imperfect way. We may not be in Alice's weird hall of mirrors, but we do (as Paul says in another of his letters) 'see through a glass, darkly' (1 Corinthians 13:12, KJV) in that we will only know or see God in a limited way in this life. Like the Ephesians, we may have experienced God powerfully in the past, but that doesn't mean our view of God doesn't shrink or enlarge as our circumstances change or as new questions or issues arise. Not one of us will go through life without pressures, challenges, loss or disappointment, and it is unsurprising that some of these circumstances and feelings might temporarily obscure or dwarf our view of who God is, or eclipse our understanding of what he might still want to do in and through us.

Like anyone reading this book, we too have experienced our share of both small and supersized challenges over the years, be that health issues, family complications, bereavement, financial problems, unfair criticism, exhaustion, betrayal, two bouts of not having anywhere to live apart from friends' spare rooms, and inevitable seasons of stress, sadness or disappointment. Alongside these, we have navigated the practical challenges and the continual sense of loss surrounding Mark's decreasing eyesight due to a degenerative inherited condition.[2] Disability is never easy to come to terms with, and in a very literal sense, blindness has brought about a huge shift in perspective for each of us, as we have often spoken or written about over the years.

We share these realities not because we are special in any way – quite the reverse, in fact! It is because we are not unusual at all. Facing tests and trials in life is not unusual and does not mean we are a failure. Indeed, biblically speaking, that is what we are to expect.[3] Every one of us will experience times of incredible joy and wonderful opportunities as well as deep chasms of sadness in our life. That is the norm.

The question, then, is whether our view of God shrinks and grows in relation to our present circumstances. I (Mark) often tell people to avoid the understandable but unhelpful tendency to confuse life and God. Life can certainly be disappointing and unfair; that does not mean God is disappointing and unfair. Life can be inconsistent and painful; that does not mean God is inconsistent or the one inflicting the pain. As our challenges enlarge at times, our view of God can unwittingly shrink as a result, because we have created a conscious or subconscious correlation between the size of our struggle and the goodness of our God. In the relatively affluent and comfortable West, we may well have adopted a mindset or worldview that says God is good because life is good. He provides for us and he cares for us, after all! But what about when the provision is delayed, or the diagnosis is depressing? Does he still care for us then?

But not everything in life that is comfortable or easy is Jesus, and not everything that is difficult is the devil. Battles and blessings are continual features of the landscape of life, which is why we need to keep focused on God's faithfulness in every season. Paul's words in this opening overture remind us that our starting point, our final destination point and presumably all the points we will stop at along the way in life need to be seen through this significant lens: God is more magnificent, wise, forgiving, gracious, glorious, loving and lavish than we will ever really know or fully comprehend. And he *never* changes.

Perhaps we need reminding of this from time to time. We really are already blessed, and we are always blessed, whatever our circumstances. As Paul says here in Ephesians 1:3, 'Praise be to the God and Father of our Lord Jesus Christ, who has blessed us in the heavenly realms with every spiritual blessing in Christ.'

This is a big-picture blessing! It is interesting to note that this phrase 'heavenly realms' is used five times in the book of Ephesians (but in no other letters), and doesn't refer to a specific place or a divine abode in the sky, but to the entire spiritual sphere that exists where Christ reigns supreme and we reign with him, and in which God therefore blesses us with every spiritual blessing.[4] So, every spiritual blessing in the heavenly realms is not just something we can look forward to in the future, but is something that is secured and promised for us in every circumstance and season of life – even today. God has guaranteed a life of his presence and blessing for us – his grace, our salvation and our eternal future are completely secure.

This means that however big our problems, however real our sadness, we can look up and be reassured that we have a relationship with our majestic heavenly Father, made possible through Christ and sealed with the Holy Spirit, and that is a blessing to us. So although we might not always see our challenges shrink in size as much as we'd like, when we increase our view of God, we can regain or retain a more hope-filled perspective. To be clear, this is not about denying, minimising or overlooking your reality; nor is it some kind of positive thinking or striving to summon up more faith. Rather, it is about looking up and being deeply reassured that above it all and through it all we can encounter a faithful heavenly Father who loves us and has already given us every spiritual blessing in Christ. We have much to give thanks and praise for.

Significant spiritual blessing

As we return to this opening passage, let's marvel for a few moments more at some of these spiritual blessings we have been promised. They are significant, and by highlighting these at the very start of his letter, Paul purposefully reiterated key themes to the Ephesians that should also give us cause for hope and thanksgiving.

We are chosen

Have you ever heard people tell how traumatised they were because they were never chosen for the sports team at school, often left until the very end, like leftovers that nobody wanted? A couple of things here – first, why in the world did PE teachers use this barbaric system of ritual humiliation? It's awful! But second, if every person who shares this experience is telling the truth, it's hard to believe anyone was ever picked first! Athleticism (or lack of it) aside, at one point or another we have all experienced rejection, not being chosen or being overlooked. And when individuals or people groups, ethnicities or races are oppressed, persecuted or disadvantaged, it is painful and a societal evil. Being valued, honoured or chosen is, therefore, a blessing and what God intended.

In Ephesians 1:4–6 Paul states that before the creation of the world, we were chosen – elected or predestined to be adopted as sons and daughters (the word encompasses both).[5] Now, the best theological brains throughout history have found the doctrine of election confusing and difficult, so it would be understandable if we couldn't fully wrap our minds around it either. Did I choose to follow Jesus or did God choose me first? Did I freely decide or was it decided already? What about others who have not chosen to follow? Were they, in fact, not chosen, like sports-team leftovers? The doctrine of election is a mystery and a tension that is hard to systemise or rigidly explain, and the Bible doesn't seek to resolve it for us fully.

To help us grasp this concept of election, somebody once described it as being like a sign over a doorway. On the side of the entrance it says, 'All are welcome' and on the other side looking back it says, 'You were chosen'. With God, it seems that somehow both are true. We have free will, yet God called us before the creation of the world – and not just to be servants or even friends, but to be adopted as children, surely the highest dignity God could bestow upon us, with all the privileges, responsibilities and relational access that adoption confers, both in Roman law and to us now. And being adopted not only means being chosen and loved, but also having a completely new legal status. Paul wanted his readers to understand that they have been brought into God's family and this security is utterly unshakeable.[6] We are his chosen people.

Indeed, Paul is connecting his readers to this much wider and larger narrative of God's salvation story. As we know from the book of Genesis, humankind rebelled in the garden of Eden, and this sin disconnected us from our Creator. God then chose Abraham, Isaac and Jacob 'to be bearers of his promised salvation for the world',[7] and the Jewish people considered themselves to be God's chosen people and precious possession (Deuteronomy 7:6). Paul's readers, who were primarily Gentiles (non-Jewish), were being both pointed towards and encompassed by and embraced into the greater story of all believers, Jews *and* Gentiles, who are now chosen to be part of the fulfilment of God's ancient plan and purpose.[8]

We are in Christ

The opening verses of Ephesians also reveal God as Trinity, clearly referring to Father, Son and Holy Spirit. Indeed, in the first fourteen verses of this letter, Jesus Christ is mentioned by name or title or pronoun no fewer than fifteen times, and the phrase 'in Christ' (or 'in him') occurs eleven times.[9] This is significant. As theologian John Stott explains, 'Formerly we were "in Adam", belonging to the old fallen humanity; now we are "in Christ", belonging to the new redeemed humanity.'[10] It is only *in Christ* that we have been blessed and chosen, that we have been given grace, that we become God's new-covenant chosen possession, and that we are part of God's plan to unite all things for his glory. It is not down to our hard work, great ideas, adherence to the law, or even the hours we spend praying or serving. It is being in Christ that makes the difference.

How important it is to keep Jesus at the centre of our lives. I remember when I (Cathy) became a Christian at university, despite not having been brought up as a churchgoer at all. I was spiritually curious and was open to the idea of there being a God or a higher power, and this curiosity increased as I began to learn about Jesus. But being curious was not enough. Even being convinced of the truth of Christ was not enough. It was only when I took the step of faith to receive Christ that I entered into his promises as one of his children called out for his purposes. What a privilege and a joy it was then, and it still is now, decades later! We are blessed because we are in Christ, and he dwells in us.

We are redeemed

I'm sure all our readers are very law-abiding citizens, but even you may have received a parking fine at some point in your life. Have you, though, ever been let off from paying a parking fine? (Pretty rare!) Or have you ever been forgiven for a mistake or set free early from a school detention back in the day? It's a great feeling. There is probably nothing more marvellous than being shown undeserved grace or unmerited kindness in a situation where we can't redeem ourselves.

And yet in Ephesians 1:7–8 we read that a deliverance, or ransom, has been paid for us, and the word Paul used to describe this is a ransom paid for a prisoner of war or a slave being set free, who could never free themselves. What a powerful truth it is that the death and resurrection of Jesus liberates us where we could never free ourselves. We are utterly powerless to find forgiveness and freedom from our sin – it separates us from God, no matter how hard we try. But God made it possible through Jesus. He paid the price, or the ransom, for us.

But there is another big-picture perspective at play here. The words Paul used also echoed back to God's deliverance of the children of Israel in Egypt and God's continual rescuing of his people in times of trouble.[11] N. T. Wright reminds us that the original readers of this letter would have immediately recalled the Jewish Passover story, when 'the angel of death came through the land of Egypt, and the blood of the lamb sprinkled on the doorposts rescued the Israelites from the judgement that would otherwise have fallen on them'.[12] It is hard to overstate the significance of this and the promise in Exodus 6:6–8 that God would be their God and they would be his people, whom he rescued. The identity of the Jewish people was built on this hugely significant moment. But for them and for us, says Wright, 'Forgiveness of sins is the real "deliverance" from the real slavemaster',[13] and our story is now one where we too recall how Jesus has rescued and redeemed us and set us free to live for him – we are all now his people and he is our God.

We probably don't talk or preach enough about this. Perhaps we don't think we are all that bad or sinful, or maybe we've even slightly taken God's amazing grace, redemption and rescue for granted. Perhaps we, the Church, need to look up again and grasp this truth more fully in order to live in the richness of it. As Paul says elsewhere, 'It is for freedom that Christ has set us free (Galatians 5:1). Freedom and deliverance are good news – and news worth sharing. We have been redeemed and set free!

We have revelation

Allow us to make a confession. We tend to exercise a little caution when well-meaning but enthusiastic Christians apparently have a hotline to God so hectic that they seem to know exactly what God is thinking and saying in every situation. Perhaps the Almighty is just far chattier to them than he is to us! That said (and humour aside), we are equally mistaken if we think that God is a silent God, or a heavenly Father who doesn't want to give revelation or insight. Ephesians 1:8–9 declares that he gives wisdom and understanding, and they reveal the mystery of his will, which he purposed in Christ.

Paul is reminding his readers here that through Jesus' victory on the cross, one of the riches of grace that we receive is access to the mysteries of God, leading to the fulfilment of his purposes. This doesn't mean that God is constantly downloading instructions into our heads. But it does mean that as we read God's word, as we pray, worship, share and learn with other believers, engage in spiritual disciplines[14] and stay attentive to the nudges of the Holy Spirit,[15] we will become increasingly immersed in the way of Jesus and therefore able to discern God's wisdom.

In James 1:5 we are also instructed to ask God for wisdom if we lack it. Probably all of us could do with more wisdom, so it is important that we remember to ask for it. God will encourage us, remind us, help us, prompt us and direct us in all areas of life – be that at home, at work, in our relationships or in our most challenging circumstances. God has wonderfully given us access to his wisdom and understanding – not to solve all our problems but to enable us to abide in him and navigate life with him, so that his kingdom might come and his will might be done, and ultimately all things will be brought to unity under Christ.[16]

We are sealed with the Holy Spirit

Back in the days of yore (and you may have seen this depicted in a film), a member of the nobility would take a document and drip some hot wax onto it. They would then create an imprint from a ring or make a ruler's mark where the wax would not only seal the document but also authenticate it. When that document was then passed on, both the carrier and the intended recipient would see the seal and have confidence in the authority it represented.

While it is possible to place a wax seal like this on something externally, the Holy Spirit is a mark of ownership and authenticity on our hearts. We are God's own people, and our salvation, together with our ability to live empowered and fruitful lives in unity with others, is only possible because of the work of the Holy Spirit who has been given to us. He is our promise (Ephesians 1:13), and his seal authenticates the transforming work of God in our lives.

But more than this, Paul says that the Holy Spirit is not only a promised seal, but also a guarantee, deposit or pledge (v. 14). Maybe you have paid a deposit or put a down payment on a washing machine or even a house in the past. When you signed that piece of paper (or ticked the screen!), you entered a transaction for a promised purchase that you then had to fulfil. This theological metaphor used by Paul gives us a guaranteed eternal hope; the first instalment or down payment of the Holy Spirit not only promises our final inheritance as his redeemed possession (v. 14), but wonderfully also gives us a foretaste of it now.[17]

Big-picture prayers

Attempting to grapple with these significant and perspective-shifting blessings will inevitably shape how we approach God. The more fully we see God and grow in our understanding of who he is and how he loves and rescues us, the more likely we are to approach him confidently and authentically in prayer.

When our daughters were small, they were convinced that Mark could solve every problem and answer every question. Their dad was almost always the one they came to expectantly for insights, decisions or explanations, be that about the Tudors, the stars visible in the sky or which teddy bear should go to camp! There was one memorable day when we were doing something special as a family, but the weather forecast was terrible. Our younger daughter looked up confidently and said, 'Don't worry. Daddy can fix it!' Her confidence in Mark's meteorological powers was slightly over-optimistic, but her belief in her father was touching. Perhaps this is why Jesus commended a child-like faith. When a child looks up at a parent they love and trust, they do so with expectation and optimism, believing that their father or mother will be attentive and willing in response. Our heavenly Father is greater than any flawed human parent could be, and we can trust that he is always ready and willing to listen and to spend time with us.

Reading Paul's opening 'overture', we get a clear and powerful sense of his incredible trust and confidence in who God is. But beyond Paul's initial exhortation to look up in this opening paragraph, there are two great and often-quoted prayers in Ephesians that are full of passion and pastoral care towards the people he is writing to. We can clearly see that when Paul looks up in prayer, he does so at a glorious Father (1:17) who gives a glorious inheritance (1:18) and who strengthens us out of his glorious riches (3:16) to the praise of his glorious grace (1:6) for his praise and glory for ever and ever (3:20). What an evocative and wholehearted word 'glorious' is! Paul doesn't see God as a half-interested, stingy or powerless deity. No, Paul is praying to the 'immeasurably more' God (3:20) with 'incomparably great power' (1:19), whose love 'surpasses knowledge' (3:19). Glorious indeed!

It is worth reading these two magnificent prayers side by side.

I keep asking that the God of our Lord Jesus Christ, the glorious Father, may give you the Spirit of wisdom and revelation, so that you may know him better. I pray that the eyes of your heart may be enlightened in order that you may know the hope to which he has called you, the riches of his glorious inheritance in his holy people, and his incomparably great power for us who believe. That power is the same as the

mighty strength he exerted when he raised Christ from the dead and seated him at his right hand in the heavenly realms, far above all rule and authority, power and dominion, and every name that is invoked, not only in the present age but also in the one to come. And God placed all things under his feet and appointed him to be head over everything for the church, which is his body, the fullness of him who fills everything in every way.
(Ephesians 1:17–23)

For this reason I kneel before the Father, from whom every family in heaven and on earth derives its name. I pray that out of his glorious riches he may strengthen you with power through his Spirit in your inner being, so that Christ may dwell in your hearts through faith. And I pray that you, being rooted and established in love, may have power, together with all the Lord's holy people, to grasp how wide and long and high and deep is the love of Christ, and to know this love that surpasses knowledge – that you may be filled to the measure of all the fullness of God.

Now to him who is able to do immeasurably more than all we ask or imagine, according to his power that is at work within us, to him be glory in the church and in Christ Jesus throughout all generations, for ever and ever! Amen.
(Ephesians 3:14–21)

What stirring and inspiring prayers!

Paul's words weave together threads of petition and praise, blessing and benediction, intercession and eager expectation. They reveal his belief in God's incomparably great power, but also in his love that passes knowledge and understanding. He is aware of his desperate need for God, but continually points back to Jesus and his glory. Indeed, what strikes me (Mark) is the focus of these prayers. Rather than praying about their circumstances or troubles, Paul consistently prays that his readers might have a bigger view of God and his power. He prays that they might be given the Spirit of wisdom and revelation in order to know him better (1:17); that the eyes of their hearts might be enlightened so they will know the hope in which they are called; that they will give thanks for the riches of his glorious inheritance and his incomparably great power (vv. 18–19). Then in chapter 3 he prays for them to be internally reinforced so that Christ may dwell in their hearts (vv. 16–17); that they might have the power to grasp how wide, long, high and deep is the love of Christ (v. 18) and they will be filled to the measure of all the fullness of God (v. 19). In essence, Paul prays that the believers' perspective will be dominated and illuminated by an enlarged view of a very big God.

One thing is certainly striking: Paul was a passionate man of prayer. He wasn't praying because his church leader had badgered him to go to a meeting. He wasn't praying because he thought he ought to and felt guilty about it. And he didn't fall into the trap of thinking that prayer and action are somehow separated from one another – let's not forget he was writing these prayers in prison because of the boldness of his actions! Paul knew that his strength was rooted and established in Christ's love, and that God was the source of power who enabled his writing, preaching, pastoral work and travelling, or his waiting in chains.

Prayer makes a difference. It is the fuel for our living and perhaps one of the most essential and often undervalued activities in our lives. Prayer is never a waste of time, as Jesus modelled again and again. Prayer might take many forms and might be expressed in many ways, but God always hears the prayer of one of his children. On one hand, we don't need to impress God with fancy words, but neither should we underestimate the potency of our most simple and heartfelt prayers. And as we take time to come into our Father's presence, it is as if we come home; we shake off the pressures of the world and realign ourselves again with heaven. Unsurprisingly, our weary souls find rest and our perspective shifts as a result.

Unlike Paul, we are probably not praying in prison, but whatever life looks like for us today, our need for God is no less. Many of us have limitations or frustrations; we may be stressed or depressed, we are often overworked and constantly bombarded by the world's message that hope and fulfilment are to be found in money, gratification and power. We are also living in a digitally immersed world, with fewer boundaries than ever before between work, home and family, and a 24/7 news cycle that not only informs but often overwhelms us with calamity after catastrophe, constantly alerting us to global issues that are often beyond our ability to understand or control. Closer to home, many of us are dealing with financial challenges, difficult diagnoses or painful relationships. Navigating the pathway of life can be wonderful, but it can also be confusing and exhausting sometimes. Which is why where we look matters.

Looking in the right direction

Downward

In difficult seasons, when we are weighed down or overwhelmed, our world often becomes smaller, and the bigger picture might seem out of focus or even unmanageable. It is understandable, really. We can all identify those heavy or extremely busy times when we keep our head down and keep going. We often end up withdrawing or fixating on certain issues just to cope. Looking up might seem impossible. We may well need to be reminded that God cares about our situation and walks with us a step at a time through valleys, but he doesn't want us to set up a permanent camp there. Choosing to look up again, with a prayer or worship song for example, will give us hope that there is a bigger horizon and a path ahead, while also reassuring us that in many cases 'This too shall pass'.

Outward

These days, it seems apparently normal and even encouraged to compare ourselves and to compete with others. Social media has obviously supersized this tendency to look around, meaning we can be tempted to follow, admire and elevate others (while often diminishing ourselves in the process). Although what we are seeing is an airbrushed and edited version of their lives, we might sometimes look at the lifestyle, beauty or success of others and subconsciously use them as a benchmark for how we are living our life. Looking outwards might also mean looking primarily to others for approval, promotion, affirmation or 'likes'. But ultimately this doesn't work – our job can't give us everything we need and neither can any other imperfect person. Although it *is* good to look around for fellowship, support and prayer, and for people to love and serve, that God-given capacity for community becomes warped or corrupted when we look around in order to find our identity and purpose – which is only found in God.

Inward

It is not a bad thing to be self-aware, and the rise in understanding about our mental health, emotional well-being and resilience is significant and needed. It is incredibly important for us to know our limits,[18] and to understand when our limits and boundaries are being breached or when our energy tank is running dry. But while inner strength is important, there will always be a limit to self-help. We can't rescue ourselves by ourselves. We were not designed to live in disconnection – from others or from God. Introspection can be positive, but isolation is not. The Bible is clear that none of us will ever have all the answers or all the resources; we together are a body, a family and a chosen people, and we need God's help.

Upward

Rather than downward, outward or inward, then, we can look upward, as Paul did, and cultivate the habit of lifting our eyes to where our help comes from: the Lord, the Maker of heaven and earth (Psalm 121). There is only one way we will be sustained, empowered and set free, and that is by looking to God. When we lift our eyes to him, when we pray, worship or marvel at God's word or his handiwork in creation, we are reminded of his majesty, and we are reassured that we have already received so much in Christ. He really is enough for us. He has lavished on us everything we need, spiritually speaking. God can see far beyond the horizon of whatever we are currently facing, and as we look up we will find the courage and confidence to live for Christ and his glory.

God is so much bigger than we think! We'd encourage you to read those two prayers from Ephesians again and make them your own. Whatever the challenge or opportunity before you, he is bigger. Whatever you have overcome and however big your fears or dreams for the future might be, he is stronger, and his love is wider, longer, higher and deeper than you could ever know. Our awesome Creator God knew you before the beginning of time, and his vast love for you reaches beyond time; you are secure – you are his and you are found in him. If God can do immeasurably more than we can ask or imagine, we can look up and pray even for immeasurably more imagination. We therefore don't need to give or serve in order to get; we give because we already have what we need. Knowing we are rooted and established in love, and that God's glorious grace is lavished upon us with every spiritual blessing in Christ, we can serve this broken world, our colleagues, our family and the neighbours in our street, because God is more powerful and loving than we could ever be.

It is as we look up that we gain the vision, the confidence and the perspective we need each day. And as we keep our eyes fixed on our glorious King of kings, he will enable us to fully live a life worthy of the calling we have received. As a great hymn writer once put it:

Be Thou my Vision, O Lord of my heart;
be all else but naught to me, save that Thou art;
be Thou my best thought, in the day and the night,
both waking and sleeping, Thy presence my light.
(Trans. Mary E. Byrne, 1880–1931)

Look up – working it out

Reflect

Reflect on your spiritual blessings.

Spend a few moments giving thanks for your spiritual blessings. What has God done for you in and through Jesus? Read Ephesians 1:3–14 again and try writing your own unpunctuated prayer of praise!

Recalibrate

Why not have a vision check? Where are you looking?

Consider where you tend to focus the most, especially in times of trial or challenge. Where do you tend to look for comfort, validation, approval, hope, wisdom or confidence? Ask yourself:

- Do I look down? Do I get buried in work or other distractions, or allow my problems to obscure everything else? When do I do this most? How else could I find peace?
- Do I look around? Do I seek validation or approval from others? Do I look predominantly to a job or person to provide and

satisfy? What ways of looking around are more positive and life-giving?

- Do I look in? Do I comfort myself in positive or unhelpful ways? Do I rely on my own resources beyond what is reasonable? What are my limits?
- Do I look up? How established are my patterns of worship, prayer, reading the Bible or serving, for example? How instinctively do I speak to God or seek his wisdom or acknowledge his blessing?

Looking up intentionally

What helps you to look up and consider God's vast power and love? What causes you to pause in awe and wonder? How could you cultivate this, and how might it encourage you to pray? Ideas might include:

- walking in nature – forests, fields, rivers, mountains or the local park;
- exploring science and the cosmos (the universe is huge, but atoms are so small!);
- listening to music – melodies and scores often express the inexpressible;
- studying – digging deeper into Scripture, theology or other fields that inspire;
- engaging in creative pursuits – poetry, craft, painting, woodwork – we have a Creator God, after all;
- memorising Psalm 8 or another section of the Bible that declares God's glory.

Rejoice

Heavenly Father,

I thank you for your glorious riches, which strengthen me with power in my inner being. I thank you that Christ dwells in my heart through faith, and I am rooted and established in your love. Help me to look primarily to you, the giver of all good things, and to be thankful for every spiritual blessing you have given me. I pray today I would grasp again your love that passes all knowledge, and I would look to you and see you at work in every circumstance.

Amen.

2

Wake up

You have been given an entirely new life

Have you ever been unexpectedly upgraded on a plane journey? We sadly haven't, but our younger daughter has. While travelling to Sierra Leone in West Africa for a church partnership visit with a charity, she was upgraded to business class, and as you can imagine she was delighted! She revelled in telling us about her extra-wide seat, which folded out flat to make a bed, the gadgets and games she could play with, the fancy food with (wait for it) proper cutlery – basically a completely different experience from the economy level we have always known. I confess that I (Mark) have shamelessly attempted to get upgraded in the past. I have smiled sweetly at the check-in staff, emphasised the Revd title in my name (which I never normally use) and dressed smartly. I've even wondered if the fact that I am blind might sway the cabin crew. But no. Economy it is – which is what I've paid for, after all.

Back on terra firma, an upgrade we are more likely to experience is a new and improved gadget – a laptop or a phone, for example. Fundamentally, our newer version is still the same as the older one, but the upgrade (once you have worked out how to use it) does it all faster and more easily, and looks shinier.

It is easy to transfer this upgrade mindset to our spiritual lives, if we are not careful. Perhaps in our efforts to make our faith relevant and accessible (no bad thing and no judgement implied here), some of our messages and church social media posts may give the impression that church is mainly a great lifestyle choice, with a better and nicer sense of community and some excellent social gatherings. We might also inadvertently reduce discipleship to being a bit more loving, praying for a few minutes more or being a nicer person who knows they need to deal with their road-rage issues. None of these things are bad. In fact, they are all very good. The trouble is, there are plenty of nice, mindful, altruistic people who have no faith whatsoever. So what difference does being a Christian make?

Paul, in this letter to the Ephesians,[1] is suggesting something far more radical and fundamental than a life upgrade. After all, he was not imprisoned for a lifestyle hack, for tweaking his beliefs or for eating quiche at a church picnic! Paul had become convinced of and was now sharing a significant, challenging and slightly mind-blowing truth: that we were once dead and now we are 'up and alive' in Christ; we are transformed completely and eternally because of Jesus.

We are not upgraded in Christ; we are resurrected!

God's purpose is not to make all things slightly better;
God is making all things new
(Revelation 21:5).

No wonder Paul was compelled to share what he believed at all costs. He'd once had all the first-class status and prestige he could ever want as a respected Pharisee who persecuted Christians, but now he was convinced of the truth of Jesus; now he was spiritually *alive*, and he wanted to make that truth as clear as possible to others.

Wake up to a new status

It is certainly a stark statement to say that we were once dead and now we are alive. But Paul's use of these opposing or contrasting truths is deliberate and illuminating. We will never understand or appreciate what it is to be truly alive (and living in the fullness of God) if we don't first understand or appreciate the implications of being spiritually dead. Furthermore, this revelation affects our mission. Why would we see the point of sharing our faith, of evangelism or mission, if we were not convinced we had a message that raises dead people to life? There's no urgency in offering a bit of an upgrade.

But Paul makes it clear that new life is exactly what God offers. He first explains (at the end of Ephesians 1) that Jesus was dead, but God raised him to life and exalted him, then he immediately mirrors that (at the start of chapter 2) to say that we were also dead, but God raised us to life and exalted us. Here are some of Paul's words again: 'As for you, you were dead in your transgressions and sins' (Ephesians 2:1), and 'But because of his great love for us, God, who is rich in mercy, made us alive with Christ even when we were dead in transgressions' (2:4–5).

Perhaps the challenge for many of us here is that this binary, polarised contrast is so dramatic, it can be hard to grasp or accept. Most of us don't think we are actually that bad. Sure, we roll our eyes at our boss behind their back sometimes, we once told a little fib about why we couldn't attend a party and maybe we've slightly exaggerated from time to time. But dead? That sounds a bit extreme. After all, we all know people who are worse than us, so are they more dead than us? Are they deader? Are we dead-ish? We are probably more comfortable thinking of Jesus improving us and tweaking our minor sins and transgressions than totally transforming us.

But when Paul uses this metaphor to describe the human condition, he isn't referring to some particularly horrific criminals or a specific segment of society; he is describing us all, however large or small our misdemeanours. In fact, he is using the word 'death' more factually than figuratively in the sense that this really is our spiritual condition when we are outside Christ – we are not truly alive until we are living in relationship with God our Creator.

It is interesting to discover more about the words Paul has carefully chosen when he says we are dead in our sins and trespasses. The ancient Greek word used for sin is *hamartanein* – a word that is associated with shooting and from which comes 'hamartia'. It literally means 'a miss'. So, let's imagine you have a bow and arrow, you aim and then you shoot the arrow at the target and the arrow misses. That is hamartia. Sin, then, in this context, is us failing to hit the target of God's best for our life, or missing God's standards in some way, which surely applies to every single one of us, since none of us are perfect and all of us have fallen short of God's best.[2]

The other word Paul uses here is *paraptōma*, which has been translated as 'trespasses'. This literally means 'a false step' or 'a slip' or 'a fall', and might be used to describe a person who has crossed a boundary or strayed from the right path when they could have taken the right one, or one who has slipped or fallen away from a truth they should have known.[3]

These are missteps and wrongdoings we can all relate to, and they are both active and passive – sins of omission and sins of commission, if you like. There are always things we have done wrong and things we should have done better, are there not?[4] And Paul is reminding us that this stuff matters. It is not about grading minor or major misdemeanours, spiritually speaking. It was sin that separated us from God, right back in the garden of Eden, and it was sin that the people of Israel had to atone for through the extensive sacrificial system. Paul is explaining how Jesus' death and resurrection deals with this sin problem once and for all.

It is worth reading more of this passage in a more modern translation to allow the truth to permeate our minds and souls in a fresh way.

It wasn't so long ago that you were mired in that old stagnant life of sin. You let the world, which doesn't know the first thing about living, tell you how to live. You filled your lungs

with polluted unbelief, and then exhaled disobedience. We all did it, all of us doing what we felt like doing, when we felt like doing it, all of us in the same boat. It's a wonder God didn't lose his temper and do away with the whole lot of us. Instead, immense in mercy and with an incredible love, he embraced us. He took our sin-dead lives and made us alive in Christ. He did all this on his own, with no help from us! Then he picked us up and set us down in highest heaven in company with Jesus, our Messiah.
(Ephesians 2:1–6, MSG)

The Bible can be refreshing in its realism, don't you think? In this one short passage Paul clearly paints a picture of what humankind is by nature and what we can become by grace. God knows how wayward we can all be, but he also knows all we have the capacity to be, and Paul here both 'plumbs the depths of pessimism about man, and then rises to the heights of optimism about God'.[5] No matter who we are, how successful, beautiful, kind, intelligent or hardworking we may or may not be, 'in the sphere that matters supremely (which is neither the body, nor the mind, nor the personality, but the soul)' we are not alive if we are 'blind to the glory of Jesus Christ and deaf to the voice of the Holy Spirit'.[6]

How incredible it is that not only were we raised from death to life, but we have also been seated in the heavenly realms with Jesus to know the incomparable riches of his grace (2:6–7). We have been lifted up to where we see everything differently. Almost like when a parent picks up a child and places him or her on a kitchen worktop, enabling that child to see the world from a different level and to speak face to face, we will view our surroundings differently when we know where we are seated.

As children of God we are in the privileged position of being heirs with Christ. We might not deserve that position, but that is who we are. So in our challenges, where we may sometimes feel

27

weak or overwhelmed, we are not powerless and our prayers are not unheard. Instead, we are positioned or seated with Christ, understanding that he is with us and for us. This position should not make us feel more important or arrogant as we go about our business – in fact, quite the opposite. The security of our position should mean that we are more gracious and compassionate people, who point to the hope we have in God.

Do you need to let this sink in again today?

Do you need to pause and recalibrate your soul, which tries so hard to be good enough for God?

Do you even know how alive you are in Christ?

In all honesty, maybe we all experience seasons when we sleepwalk in our faith or we become a little hazy about what Jesus has done for us. This is a good time for us all (as individuals and as a church) to wake up again and to grasp the radically powerful truth of who God has made us and called us to be: not merely a slightly better version of ourselves, but completely new, with a new status, position and purpose through Jesus.

This is far better news than a mere upgrade, isn't it? God's amazing grace is not a spiritual engine tune-up or some suggested tweaks we can make to improve our lives, or even a self-development programme. Because of God's great mercy and love, the power that raised Jesus from the dead has also made us 'up and alive'. He has changed and awakened our status from being part of the kingdom of darkness to being citizens of the kingdom of light. He saved us into a completely new life, under new rule and reign. We have been adopted into his family and redeemed from death into a place where we can know God's abundant life.

Hallelujah! What a Saviour!

Wake up to a glorious gospel

We should never lose our confidence in the gospel (or good news) and Jesus' power to transform lives. This is why every baptism service is so exciting – we are reminded that the good news really is good, and that God is still at work today, bringing new life and new hope. And while the gospel of Jesus is wonderful news for those who hear it for the first time, there is also always more to discover. As pastor and writer Tim Keller once said, 'The gospel has been described as a pool in which a toddler can wade and yet an elephant can swim. It is both simple enough to tell to a child and profound enough for the greatest minds to explore.'[7]

In reality, it can sometimes be hard to summarise 'the gospel' or what it means to be a disciple, and most of us don't claim to be theologians. But if we are thinking about God, we are indeed thinking theologically and it matters, as we will naturally embody and share what we understand the truth to be. Our thinking and our doing are inextricably linked, and our beliefs and behaviours shape one another. And with so many cultural influences around us and multifarious messages that shape our thinking every day, we need to commit to developing our critical and biblical thinking as much as possible, so that our interpretation of the gospel is as wide, full, rich and wonderful as God intends it to be.

This means it will be important to consider the impact of our culture or cultural influences, and to understand what we mean by this to begin with. Dictionary definitions of 'culture' generally describe the ideas, customs and social behaviour of a particular people or society, but we might most simply describe it as 'how we do things round here'. So, our culture is not just about the country or the era we live in, although these are clearly significant. We are also located in our families, communities (online and in-person), workplaces and churches, which all have a particular culture where certain expectations, behaviours, values, traditions and beliefs are

29

either tolerated, celebrated or sidelined. We all live in, accept and replicate certain cultural norms and, knowingly or not, we are shaped by the people and places we are immersed in. Unsurprisingly, then, our societal norms, our media intake, our background, our race or gender, our theological and denominational distinctives and our particular settings and personal experiences all shape how we understand and therefore share the good news about Jesus. So the challenge for us all is one of hermeneutics – we need to accept the lenses through which we see, and then seek to understand and interpret the Bible to find its original meaning in order to apply and embody its truth today in our context.

Accepting that our understanding might not always be complete or even correct is a good thing – there is always more to learn! This is certainly true when we consider both the simplicity and the profundity of the gospel. Below, then, are some forms or versions of the gospel that you might recognise. They may contain some important elements of truth, but they don't reveal the good news in all its fullness. Some awareness and critique of these versions is helpful, because we don't want to preach or accept a skewed or incomplete gospel that might lead us and others away from God's plan rather than inviting us to join it.

A forgiveness-only gospel

This version of the good news zooms in on the fact that Jesus came, died and rose again to forgive our sins and give us eternal life. Therefore it focuses particularly on moments of conversion. Of course, there is important truth here and it is not to be minimised, but a too-narrow focus on one prayer could inadvertently give the impression that if we just say the right words then we are all sorted, thereby sidestepping the issue of discipleship or the wider good news that Jesus promises the Holy Spirit will help us to live for him and bring hope to others. When we are saved, we are called both individually and communally into God's redemptive plan to share our hope in Christ, but also to care about poverty, injustice and so on. We are 'God's handiwork, created in Christ Jesus to do good works, which God prepared in advance for us to do' (Ephesians 2:10), so being a disciple of Jesus involves not just praying one prayer on one day, but following him, knowing him and sharing his love, every day.

A legalistic gospel

This is a lens of understanding that emphasises knowing or believing the right theological things. Now, believing the right things is important, as we have said, but we could slide down a slippery slope if we become preoccupied with our beliefs and opinions over and above our own behaviour, meaning the two somehow become separated. It is entirely possible to be very clear about our beliefs but to live a less-than-holy life. Therefore, this stance can also become very dogmatic or legalistic about certain behaviours, emphasising duty and what we *should* do rather than grace and what we are *empowered* to do by the Holy Spirit. If we are honest, it is all too easy to slip into judging the behaviour, activity levels or theology of others, or to make assumptions about those who believe different things from us on secondary issues. While truth matters, we need to make sure we don't settle for legalistic thinking.

A works gospel

This mindset is all about the importance of your good works. Of course good works are good, but (and maybe some of us need to hear this again today) we cannot ever earn grace from God. We are not saved by fulfilling expectations or dutifully ticking a spiritual to-do list or working hard for Jesus. We are saved by grace alone, or *sola gratia*. It is only because of God's unmerited favour that we are forgiven and set free. And then, because of this grace, we willingly serve others and make a difference in the world.[8]

This is such an important distinction. Deep down, some of us think that God (and others) might approve of us more if we do more, sign up for more and pray more. These might all be great things to do, but let's not forget that we are loved already, and Jesus has done enough for us. We cannot earn God's love, because he already loves us completely and unconditionally.

A prosperity gospel

While the more extreme versions of this might involve TV preachers promising health and wealth to those who give enough or have enough faith, the more subtle messages are still prevalent. As in the other 'gospels' we've looked at, there are elements of truth here – faith does make a difference, God does care about our needs, and we are told to pray for healing and provision. But God's purpose for us is not just our comfort; it is our character and Christlikeness, and being a disciple is not about building ourselves a comfortable little kingdom that uses the world's metrics of money, influence, productivity, charisma or beauty as benchmarks for success. In fact, following Jesus is a calling to lay down our life, pick up our cross and be more concerned with giving than getting. This is part of our discipleship, then: understanding that life is not a fairy tale with guaranteed happy endings in this life. There are not always instant fixes or overnight transformations as we seek to become more like Christ, following his example. As writer and pastor Eugene Peterson describes it, discipleship is more of 'a long obedience in the same direction'.[9]

As disciples, we are citizens of the upside-down kingdom with a Beatitudes perspective,[10] where those who are often the last or least are most blessed. We should definitely present our requests to our loving heavenly Father, and he may bless us with healing and meet some of our immediate needs, but 'prayer in = answer out' is never a guaranteed faith equation. In fact, this kind of gospel can lead to deep hurt, disappointment and doubt when the 'word of faith' doesn't seem to yield the longed-for results. We need to be sensitive and wise as we pray and care for one another. Thankfully, the ultimate hope that God offers us is wider, deeper and far more satisfying: life may not always be comfortable, but God is always faithful and he never leaves us.

A consumer gospel

It was once said that 'consumerism is the amniotic fluid in which we live and breathe'.[11] We are indeed immersed in a consumer worldview if we live in a modern developed nation, and none of us are immune to the influence of our culture. It permeates the way we think more than we might like to admit. We need to realise that our context can create potential blind spots in our thinking and in what we therefore determine we believe.

This is our modern world. We are targeted recipients of constant advertising, made by expert marketeers and psychologists, deployed by complex algorithms to continually express to us via every device and format possible that we have *so* many unmet needs and, yes, we *so* deserve to have those needs met. We *need* that holiday, that gadget or that car and we don't need those pesky wrinkles! And, of course, we want it all delivered NOW, be that food, products or experiences, all made possible by the internet and WiFi, which is surely the new human right we can't live without.

This is our new normal. So is it possible to sidestep this worldview and think totally differently when it comes to our faith or church? A consumerist mindset is insidious and if we are not careful it subtly manifests itself by producing disciples who will search (shop?) for a church that meets all their needs, with fabulous teaching, great children's work and excellent coffee (a necessity). And if some of those needs are not met, or if they experience discomfort, then perhaps it is time to express their disappointment and look for another church. (Please forgive this rather provocative exaggeration – except maybe first ask your church leader about how exaggerated it really is!)

More seriously, though, of course we are not all just out to get, get, get and most of us know that church is not a performance to be judged or a fancy ministry delivery system, and we want to push back against this mindset. Our beliefs about what the Church is (our ecclesiology) is important. We know that as Christians we are not called to be critics, commentators or consumers, but instead we are friends, participants, family and co-labourers, and sometimes *we* are the ones God is asking to get stuck in to make the difference we'd love to see. We are God's community on God's mission together. We may understand this, but we also know the consumerism trend is clear and it's a tough one to diagnose in ourselves when the lure to consume is so pervasive.

God does, of course, care about our needs, and being in a healthy, safe church culture where we can give and receive matters, and indeed this might sometimes mean talking about issues or even moving. Nevertheless, we should be diligent and discerning and encouraged to think biblically and realistically about what the Church is and is not. With the Holy Spirit's help, we can intentionally love, serve, encourage, give and pray wholeheartedly – an approach that is surely the antidote to consumeristic thinking.

A kingdom gospel

This form of the gospel emphasises the rule and reign of Jesus Christ over all of life, and his invitation to follow God's kingdom plan and purposes, particularly when it comes to wider corporate or systemic issues of injustice, climate, culture, racism, misogyny and so on. A kingdom theological perspective is therefore eschatological, in that it considers how we live in the 'now and not yet' of God's kingdom ushered in by Jesus, with his presence and power at work making all things new, until Jesus finally returns and brings everything to fulfilment. The kingdom of God is already here, we are living in it as his disciples empowered by the Holy Spirit, with all this means, but it won't be fully realised or consummated until Jesus returns.

Tim Keller, writing about this kingdom gospel, says that it 'reminds us that God created both the material and the spiritual, and is going to redeem both the material and the spiritual. The things that are now wrong with the material world he wants put right.'[12] We are, then, part of God's great restoration project, called to bring peace, justice, liberation, belonging and healing to a hurting and lonely world. The images we watch on the news matter. God's heart hurts when refugees flee, when children don't have enough food, when girls in Afghanistan can't go to school, when corruption takes root or people are treated differently because of the colour of their skin. God cares about our planet, our ecosystem and the people who are exploited to make our stuff. And our hearts should hurt too.

While other forms of the gospel might particularly foreground the individual's sin and salvation (potentially placing a more communal or global perspective in the background), the possible pitfall with this wider kingdom mindset is to forget that sin is still an issue, on both a systemic and an individual level, and that it ought not be overlooked.

The gospel or the good news of Jesus, then, is simple but also complicated, clear but mysterious and multifaceted. That said, it was and still is gloriously good news, on so many levels. Do we believe in a gospel that acknowledges our individuality and how God knows us and saves us from our sin for eternity? Yes! Does the Bible reveal that we are here to do good works and to make a difference and not just to receive? Yes! Does God care about our needs and the desires of our hearts? Yes! Are we saved by grace into a community and a heavenly kingdom ruled by Jesus, where his values of caring for the poor, the oppressed and the planet are a priority? Yes! Will it take the whole of our lives into eternity for us to understand and appreciate the richness of God's grace and the extent of what this all really means? Definitely, yes!

Thank God that the smallest child who trusts Jesus, the wisest academic theologian who has spent years studying the life of Christ, and all of us in between are part of this majestic but messy call to be God's people, because of God's grace. This is surely good news worth sharing.

Wake up to a new community

You may or may not be old enough to remember the popular 1980s TV series called *The A-Team*. In essence, this bunch of fugitive commandos, with their oh-so-catchy theme tune, were living undercover and hired by others to fix rather tricky situations. It must be said, this wasn't a series with sophisticated storylines. The plot in every episode followed pretty much the same formula: the A-Team discovered a problem (usually bad guys exploiting good people) and then in the process of trying to help the goodies, the team got captured and locked in some kind of warehouse, which coincidentally contained car parts, tools and welding equipment that could be used to make a vehicle that would help them escape. They would then turn the tables on the baddies and ensure everything ended happily ever after. Finally, the team leader, John 'Hannibal' Smith, would utter these legendary words: 'I love it when a plan comes together.' Oh, they certainly don't make 'em like they used to.

While we may never have exploded out of captivity in a flying tank-car-thing like the A-Team, I'm sure we've all felt that sentiment when a plan comes together, and yes, it is deeply satisfying. Even completing a crossword or Sudoku puzzle can give us a disproportionate level of gratification. And when we achieve something with others, when we pull together or we push through as a team or a family, working hard, praying together or experiencing breakthrough with somebody we care about, it is heart-warming and wonderful.

There is no way around it. When we look at the good news of the gospel and who God has created us to be, it is a together thing. The whole of Ephesians, written both to Jews and Gentiles who had come to faith, is a call to unity, to compassion, to forgiveness, to working together with our various gifts and backgrounds for the glory of God. This theme was *crucial* to the Church then and still is now. In fact, Jesus' farewell words to his friends, and his prayer for them (and us), emphasised love and unity and being one together (John 15–17). We need to wake up to God's continual call to unity of the Spirit, as it says in Ephesians 4:3–6:

Make every effort to keep the unity of the Spirit through the bond of peace. There is one body and one Spirit, just as you were called to one hope when you were called; one Lord, one faith, one baptism; one God and Father of all, who is over all and through all and in all.

Of course, we live in a culture that continually tells us freedom and fulfilment are found in individuality and doing your own thing, your own way, for your own fulfilment. And yet most of us would probably agree that our most memorable and meaningful moments are created when we are with others – be that with family, team, church or friends. We innately reveal something of the fullness and creative brilliance of God in our togetherness.

There is, however, an understandable tension between our valuable personal freedom, individuality and faith, and the undoubted riches of community and togetherness. Added to this is the problem that relationships take time, and unity takes commitment – things that are increasingly under pressure in our busy and stressed world. Indeed, human nature does not naturally roll downhill towards unity and peace; often what is required is a decision to travel uphill, to invest, to persevere and to forgive where necessary.

Which is why we need to be reminded that unity is not something we can necessarily summon up or work into being out of our own resources. Returning once again to the theme that seems to chime throughout the entire letter to the Ephesians, Paul urges us 'to live a life worthy of the calling you have received' (Ephesians 4:1). So this is not about us creating unity or manufacturing agreement somehow; rather we are *already* united in Christ, by Christ, for Christ. We are therefore called to protect this unity we have received, despite our diversity, and to love one another with God's help. Of course, we are imperfect people, and it isn't always easy, but the call is still clear.

Here are a few practical principles that might help.

Check your direction

Alongside the A-Team, in the 1980s some British and French engineers were embarking on their own real adventure with large machinery. Yes, this was the extraordinary creation of the Channel Tunnel, a 50-kilometre (31-mile) tunnel connecting Folkestone in Kent with Calais. Construction started with both sides digging towards each other, with the lowest point being 75 metres beneath the seabed. Can you imagine if they had not managed to meet in the middle?! Do you wonder how many times a day the project managers checked they were on course towards each other, recalibrating where necessary?

Meeting in the middle is not always easy, and recalibration is often necessary. In any friendship, marriage, team or ministry, it is all too easy to assume that everybody is working to plan, heading in the right direction, and that there is a natural meeting of minds, as it were. But in reality, it is easy to veer off course, to miscommunicate or to fail to check the thoughts and feelings of others around us. Communication and compromise are vital in any relationship.

Sweeping issues under the carpet or just hoping for the best is not a great option. We need to keep checking in, and making sure we are going in the right direction together if we don't want to grow apart.

OFM

I (Mark) will often mention the OFM principle in my church as it is so helpful. OFM stands for One Fact More. In any situation, we rarely have all the information, know all the circumstances or own all the facts. So when the shop assistant is grumpy with you? OFM – what if you discovered they had just been given a terrible diagnosis? What about the person who seemed to ignore you? OFM – what if they were visually impaired and didn't see you? That decision you disagree with to close a project or ministry? OFM – what if there are plans you don't know about yet for something new? Quite often there is a bigger picture and more to a person or an issue than we realise, be that in our workplace, in our church or in the news.

Unity not uniformity

Every person is unique, with their own gifts and talents. Ephesians 2:10 says we are all God's handiwork (bespoke masterpieces or works of art), created to do the good works God has planned for us. In truth, many of us find it easy to focus on our weaknesses or our lack of ability and might discount ourselves from God's plans. Likewise, many folk with disabilities, mental health challenges or additional needs might also feel sidelined or limited, and sadly the Church has not always helped in this regard. But unity is not about uniformity. We are *all* needed and treasured masterpieces, created, called and equipped to be part of God's purposes. None of us are excluded in God's kingdom! In Ephesians 4:11–13 Paul describes some of the gifts we find in the Church:

> So Christ himself gave the apostles, the prophets, the evange-
> lists, the pastors and teachers, to equip his people for works

of service, so that the body of Christ may be built up until we all reach unity in the faith and in the knowledge of the Son of God and become mature, attaining to the whole measure of the fullness of Christ.

In other parts of the Bible, we also read about gifts of leadership, hospitality, mercy, prayer, healing, faith, tongues, wisdom, administration and plenty more. God gives us all gifts for a specific purpose: to build his Church, with each person offering who they are to make a difference together for God's glory. And what about the outcome in verse 13? The body of Christ, the Church, will be built up until we all reach unity in faith, becoming mature and attaining to the whole measure of the fullness of Christ. What an incredible goal!

Resolve conflict well

Obviously, this would *never* happen in your church, but apparently occasionally Christians disagree. Our differences do throw up the odd difficulty, which the Bible does not shy away from. In fact, Jesus gives us an incredibly helpful blueprint for when we face relational conflict, in Matthew 18:15–17, and it's a great place to start in many cases. In essence, Jesus suggests that if we are ever offended or upset by somebody, we should talk directly to that person in order to restore relationship. If that doesn't work, we then ask somebody else in to help, but if that doesn't work, we might need to share with the church and potentially eventually part ways as a last resort. So often we see the exact opposite, don't we? Somebody feels a bit miffed with somebody else, they talk to other people about them, they harbour a grudge, let the resentment fester, avoid the person and never really work to restore the relationship.

To be clear, honesty can be costly, forgiveness is not easy and reconciliation is not always possible. Not every relationship is safe and not every circumstance is to be endured. Where there is abusive or controlling behaviour, the answer is to get help rather than plough through.[13] When we are exhausted or in a context where we know God is saying that it's time to move on, it could even be disobedience to stay where we are. It *is* good to be able to persevere, but it is equally good to know when we need to step down or step away. We can be loving and loyal, but we also know that relationships change over time.

The Bible is clear, however, that unity in the body of Christ matters – we are one body, one bride and one people, and ignoring issues, gossiping or leaking passive aggressive comments is not godly behaviour. Just as we teach children to be the friend they wish they had, so we adults need to keep being the friend, the volunteer, the spouse, the mentor, the leader or the encourager we wish we had. We become relationally mature when we can build and sustain strong and life-giving relationships, which inevitably means learning to deal with the difficult times as graciously and honestly as possible.

Wake up to a new way of living

Several years ago, for my (Mark's) birthday, Cathy arranged for me to visit a bird of prey sanctuary where I could experience a behind-the-scenes day with the staff who worked there. While most guests only saw the birds at a distance, watching various demonstrations from little arenas, my experience was totally different. I was allowed into the staff-only areas where I could be up close and personal with the birds, and I got to fly several of them, including a massive hawk thing (I can't remember its name!) and a tiny owl not much larger than my thumb. But the coolest thing of all was being given a glove and a hawk to carry around as we walked (OK, swaggered) around the site. Normal guests assumed I was an expert, and I confess I didn't put them straight. People even stopped me and asked if they could take pictures! I was a VIP for the day, and my change of status meant how I lived and behaved and experienced the day was totally different from those around me.

As we have said, Paul is reminding his readers that we have a new status in Christ. This is clearly *not* about swaggering or being self-important, but it *is* about being repositioned with Christ for his glory. We should walk and talk and think differently. This transformation from death to life should have an impact and people should notice the difference in us. Just read these words in Ephesians 5, where Paul uses another contrasting couplet, darkness to light. They encourage us again to wake up and live, not as the unwise but as the wise.

> For you were once darkness, but now you are light in the Lord.
> Live as children of light (for the fruit of the light consists in all
> goodness, righteousness and truth) and find out what pleases
> the Lord. Have nothing to do with the fruitless deeds of dark-
> ness, but rather expose them. It is shameful even to mention
> what the disobedient do in secret. But everything exposed by
> the light becomes visible – and everything that is illuminated
> becomes a light. This is why it is said:

> 'Wake up, sleeper,
>   rise from the dead,
>   and Christ will shine on you.'

> Be very careful, then, how you live – not as unwise but as
> wise, making the most of every opportunity, because the days
> are evil. Therefore do not be foolish, but understand what
> the Lord's will is. Do not get drunk on wine, which leads to
> debauchery. Instead, be filled with the Spirit, speaking to one
> another with psalms, hymns, and songs from the Spirit. Sing
> and make music from your heart to the Lord, always giving

thanks to God the Father for everything, in the name of our Lord Jesus Christ.
(Ephesians 5:8–20)

In other words, our spiritual awakening has consequences. Think for a moment about your workplace, your family and your neighbourhood. It should make an impact that you are alive in Christ! So how does your faith affect your attitude towards your friends online or your behaviour when you go out, or your response when you see somebody behave badly or corruptly? How far does your faith influence your choices, actions and attitudes each day? We cannot be alive and yet stand by or align ourselves with darkness and decay. We are God's people who illuminate the darkness with God's light and life and wisdom. Whether we are a politician, nurse, neighbour or parent, we are to be awake and alive and flavouring the world with the kindness and goodness of God.

It really is good news – we are awake! We have a whole new life! Thank God he did not just sign us up to a never-ending upgrade plan that we could never manage in our own strength. Instead, in his mercy, God reached out with good news that not only transforms us but brings his transformation to those around us. Let's always give thanks to God the Father for everything, in the name of our Lord Jesus Christ.

Wake up – working it out

Reflect

Reflect further on the gospel. The gospel is good news but can be hard to distil or summarise. Spend a few minutes considering the questions below. This will be helpful, because you embody and replicate what you believe.

- How would you express the good news of Jesus in a few sentences?

- How would you explain being a disciple of Jesus?[14]

Recalibrate

Read Ephesians 2:1–9 again. How confident are you about sharing your faith with others? Why does it matter? Could you run or attend an Alpha course online or in person?[15] Could you meet to pray for those who are not yet alive spiritually? Consider your response.

Ephesians 2:10 says that we are all unique masterpieces, created to do the good works God has planned for us. But do we know our strengths and gifts and how we therefore relate to others? Pastor Rick Warren suggests using the acrostic SHAPE to consider how God has uniquely made and called us:

- **Spiritual gifts** are God-empowered abilities given to believers for serving him – for example, serving, leading, giving, showing mercy, wisdom, prophecy, teaching.[16] What are yours?
- **Heart** refers to the desires, hopes, interests, ambitions, dreams and passions you have. What do you love to do and what do you care about most?
- **Abilities** are the natural talents you were born with. God wants you to do what you're able to do for his glory.
- **Personality** affects *how* and *where* you use your spiritual gifts and abilities. You'll use your gifts in different ways from anybody else. What makes you you?
- **Experiences** teach you lessons that help you mature. They also help you minister to others going through similar experiences.[17] What might these be?

Understanding our SHAPE, and the SHAPE of others, may help us to grow in unity and maturity together.

Rejoice

This prayer is based on Ephesians 5:8–20.

Thank you, Heavenly Father,
that we are no longer dead in our transgressions; we are
awake and alive with Christ.
We are no longer in darkness; we are now children of light.
We no longer collude with darkness; we illuminate and
expose the truth.
We are no longer sleeping or dead; Christ now shines on us.
We are not to be intoxicated; we are to be filled with the
Spirit.
We are no longer to be unwise or foolish; we are to walk in
God's wisdom.
We are no longer without hope; instead today we sing
together in thankfulness for everything God has done
and will do.

Amen.

3

Dress up

Your outfit needs to fit the new you

Let's kick-start this chapter by reminding ourselves again of the verse that seems to encapsulate the heart of Paul's letter to the Ephesians, where Paul urges us to 'live a life worthy of the calling you have received' (Ephesians 4:1). So, what does it mean to live a life that is worthy, and what difference does it make, particularly as we face various challenges each day?

Paul helpfully presents not one but two sets of clothes or clothing metaphors within the letter to the Ephesians. These enable us to live a life worthy of the calling we have received, but it is important to distinguish between them. In many ways, both sets of clothes equip us for different challenges and battles. One battleground we always face are the external circumstances and forces around us that so easily distract or pull us away from walking with God. But the other battleground is arguably just as influential, and it is the battle with our internal conflicts and desires.[1] We need to recognise that both external and internal influences exist, and we need to be dressed and prepared for both.

To distinguish these battles a little more clearly, allow us to paint a picture of a Mediterranean cruise we once enjoyed. We had no idea what to expect, as we had never been on a cruise before. Would it be too fancy for us? Would we feel trapped among thousands of people with no escape? Would we get seasick in the cheapest internal cabin on board? We need not have worried. We loved our week on this well-equipped ship that was a floating hotel and it took us to a new city to explore every day.

But alongside the sightseeing, one of the most notable features of a cruise is the food. Oh, gosh, the food. We could not believe the extensive buffet that was available throughout the day – and we are not talking overcooked, dried-out morsels that had been shrivelling on view for hours; this was a vast array of fresh, varied and oh-so-inviting dishes from around the world. And best of all? It was all included in the price and would be waiting there, whether we wanted it or not. This meant our pangs of hunger (or lack of them) became a total irrelevance. It became our responsibility not to waste all this expertly prepared food! We felt called and committed to appreciating the chefs' hard work. Similarly, scattered around the ship were freely available ice creams, snacks, more snacks and yet more ice creams. After all, one might get peckish between buffet meals.

Unsurprisingly, in our attempts to not see food go to waste, it instead went to our waists! Indeed, the constant and extensive array of food was almost impossible to resist. Temptation was inescapable.

You may or may not have been on a cruise, but you might have experienced something similar at an all-you-can-eat breakfast in a hotel or restaurant. Whereas at home you are perfectly satisfied with a piece of toast, suddenly when presented with three counter-tops of options, you discover an appetite for a full English breakfast, some pastries, some fruit and yoghurt (something healthy) and maybe a couple of muffins to stash in your pocket for later. Or is this just us?

In a buffet situation, we are presented with those two battlefields: external and internal.[2] External forces have temptingly laid out excess food for us to consume, and the pressure is applied, willing us and even expecting us to indulge. But internally we also fight a battle, as we can choose how much we take or don't take, when enough is enough and what willpower we exert. After all, we don't *have* to pile up our plates. Similarly, in hundreds of ways, we make all kinds of choices each day, and those choices may define our health and our life in many ways.

Understanding that there are always these battles helps us to be aware and to prepare accordingly, because life is constantly full of challenges and battles (as well as blessings and opportunities!). Most of us face circumstances we would not have chosen and pressures we sometimes wonder if we can cope with. It might be our health, our work, our relationships or just living in a culture with relentless news and social media, which adds stress, anxiety, temptation and false expectations daily. But, on the internal front, we can all be our own worst enemy at times too. We know we should speak kindly, be patient, spend less, scroll less, pray more or care more, but our selfish nature or even just feeling tired, down or bored can trip us up. We can't make these pressures disappear, but we can be prepared for the battles we face.

Take off and put on (Ephesians 4:17–32)

Let's take our internal world first. Our character matters to God, and attributes such as integrity, kindness, holiness and honesty are hallmarks of a Christlike person and a Jesus-honouring Church. If we want to create a healthy culture, both personally and together in our churches, we must be not only mindful but also intentional about what we tolerate, cultivate and celebrate. If, as we have already said, culture could be described as 'how we do things round here', then certain attitudes and behaviours should be pruned while others should be cultivated and honoured. After all, there are ways to deal with problems, to speak (and text and email!) wisely, to govern diligently, to parent kindly or to build one another up rather than tear one another down.

Of course, we live in a culture where freedom is loosely defined as doing whatever we want (as long as it doesn't appear to hurt others), without limitation. And yet, as society continues to pursue excess and self-fulfilment, so it also experiences increased loneliness, disconnection and inequality. Freedom, then, is far more than doing whatever we want whenever we want to. Freedom is understanding we do not need to be enslaved by our desires, or culture's messages about our need for unlimited choice. We are free, as countercultural as it may sound, to deny ourselves, to discipline our thinking and to realign our priorities and discover a renewed thirst and hunger for the righteousness of Jesus in the process.

When Paul teaches about moral ethics or holy living or 'how we do things round here in Christ' he is encouraging us to think about living with integrity and authenticity in our faith. Also, for Paul, this is never just a personal thing; it is the Church being the body of Christ (4:15), where Christ is the head. Any instructions that are applied individually are inextricably linked to how we live together in unity as a community of mature believers who are able to speak truth in love and to grow in love as each does its work (4:16). Our goal is not just personal piety, or to be a good moral, ethical citizen in a vacuum; instead, it is about all of us working it out together, which is far more challenging!

To this end, in Ephesians 4 we are presented with several negative characteristics to take off, and a corresponding and contrasting positive to put on instead. This re-clothing process is significant. Discipleship is not just striving to adopt or put on new thinking like some kind of behavioural sticking plaster placed over who we once were. We cannot just cover, mask or skirt over the issues in our old life; we need a Saviour to help us take off the old and then put on what he has provided for us. As one commentator put it, 'It is nothing less than putting off our old humanity like a rotten garment and putting on like clean clothing the new humanity recreated in God's image.'[3]

49

So, as we shall see, we are encouraged to consider what we are wearing. Just as we fully understand that we would wear one sort of outfit for a wedding, another for a job interview and something else entirely for the beach, or just as we understand that a doctor wears different attire from a gardener, or a soldier wears a uniform until they retire and change into 'civvies', similarly, then, we should wear different and new clothing as we leave behind one life and embrace a new one. Our character garments need to fit our new identity in Christ.

In effect, Paul is unpacking his death-to-life theology further and explaining that since as Christians we turned away from our past and our old nature, we logically also have to put away the practices that belong to the life we have rejected. There is supposed to be a radical difference between life without Christ and life with. Unholiness and holiness are not compatible – a truth it is perhaps possible to forget or overlook in our incredibly permissive culture.

Let's read Paul's words and ask God to speak to us today in our context:

So I tell you this, and insist on it in the Lord, that you must no longer live as the Gentiles do, in the futility of their thinking. They are darkened in their understanding and separated from the life of God because of the ignorance that is in them due to the hardening of their hearts. Having lost all sensitivity, they have given themselves over to sensuality so as to indulge in every kind of impurity, and they are full of greed.

That, however, is not the way of life you learned when you heard about Christ and were taught in him in accordance with the truth that is in Jesus. You were taught, with regard to your former way of life, to put off your old self, which is being corrupted by its deceitful desires; to be made new in the attitude of your minds; and to put on the new self, created to be like God in true righteousness and holiness.

Therefore each of you must put off falsehood and speak truthfully to your neighbour, for we are all members of one body. 'In your anger do not sin': do not let the sun go down while you are still angry, and do not give the devil a foothold. Anyone who has been stealing must steal no longer, but must work, doing something useful with their own hands, that they may have something to share with those in need.

Do not let any unwholesome talk come out of your mouths, but only what is helpful for building others up according to their needs, that it may benefit those who listen. And do not grieve the Holy Spirit of God, with whom you were sealed for the day of redemption. Get rid of all bitterness, rage and anger, brawling and slander, along with every form of malice. Be kind and compassionate to one another, forgiving each other, just as in Christ God forgave you.

(Ephesians 4:17–32)

Here, then, we have six sets of corresponding 'clothing' to discard and to put on. Humanity appears to be pretty consistent, whichever century we live in – we have cravings and desires we long to satisfy: success, money, power, ambition, accumulation, physical intimacy, approval or any number of other things. People are always people, trying to satisfy infinite desires with finite means that often just draw us yet further from the love of God, which we ultimately need most of all.

So, Paul writes to insist – not to suggest (v. 17) – that Christians no longer live like those who are futile in their thinking, with their hearts hardened by their ignorance. Strong words from Paul. In fact, this 'hardening' (*pōrōsis*) is a word that might be used to describe a callus that forms on a broken bone, knitting together and hardening in a way that deadens any sensation or feeling.[4] The implication is clear: when we continue to sin or to justify ourselves in destructive behaviours, our hearts can easily become callused, hardened or insensitive to the Holy Spirit's whispers.

But the good news is that we can think differently. In fact, Paul highlights the importance of our thinking and our understanding of the truth, because, as Jesus himself said, the truth will set us free (John 8:32). Understanding who we are in Christ liberates, redefines and refines us. Ignorance is not really bliss at all – it leads us to making unwise choices and to tolerating or rationalising all kinds of corruption and compromise.

So, what are we to take off and to put on?

1 Take off falsehood/Put on truth (4:25)

This isn't just about avoiding little white lies; it is also about denying the lies of the world and sharing the truth about Jesus. Being people of the truth means we should be known for our truth-telling, honesty, reliability and trustworthiness. In our workplaces, in our neighbourhood and in our families, unity is only ever built on trust, which is founded on the truth. So wherever there are secrets, lies or silence, or where the truth is withheld, unity, fellowship and trust are undermined. We are called to speak the truth in love (4:15), but the truth is vital as well as love.

2 Take off anger/Put on righteousness (4:26–27)

There is a clear indication here that we can be 'angry' and yet not sin. We can be righteously outraged, which means we will not tolerate injustice, oppression or slander; we can refuse to be apathetic about corruption, neglect or toxic behaviour. But, as Paul says, we need to be aware that the evil one would love to exploit our righteous frustration, provoking us towards hatred, rage, disunity or even violence. It's a fine line, which is why we need to keep short accounts, dealing with issues quickly, not allowing our angry feelings to fester or cause dissension.

3 Take off stealing/Put on contributing (4:28)

We might not be a thief or a burglar, but we can still waste others' time, fiddle expenses or behave dishonestly for our own ends. Instead, we are to work honestly, to contribute, to give and to care for others.

4 Take off unwholesome talk/Put on edifying words (4:29–30)

Our speech is powerful. When Paul writes about unwholesome talk, the word he uses denotes rottenness.[5] Whether that is unkindness, lies, gossip or putting others down on social media, words that are rotten lead to decay and death, whereas edifying words build up and impart grace. Jesus says, 'For the mouth speaks what the heart is full of' (Luke 6:45), and if we are a new creation, our heart and our words should reflect that. It should deeply trouble us that the Holy Spirit is grieved by words that demonstrate unholiness and disunity.

5 Take off bitterness/Put on compassion (4:31 – 5:2)

Paul gives us a whole list of actions and attitudes to take off: bitterness, rage, anger, brawling, malice or ill intent towards others, which might also include speaking behind people's backs, wishing the worst for others or harbouring grudges, for example. Instead, we should be known for kindness, compassion, tender-heartedness, forgiveness and acting with grace as we imitate Jesus, who gave himself up for us. This is not always easy, but possible when we live empowered by the Spirit.

6 Take off impurity/Put on thankfulness (5:3–4)

Impurity, sexual immorality and greed have no place in our new wardrobe, because they are improper garments for us. The words here imply lust, indulgence and any kind of talk or activity that gives in to those desires. Since the goddess Diana was regarded as a fertility goddess, with sexual rituals probably associated with her worship, Paul is calling for higher standards. And in our culture, where pornography, obscene images, sexualised performances and instant gratification via apps are ubiquitous, Scripture calls us to something different too. Instead, we are to be *thankful* for intimacy and committed relationships that don't degrade or cheapen a gift from God. Faithfulness, singleness, marriage and holiness in the context of sexuality are often difficult areas for the Church, with complex issues that are both pastoral and theological in nature. But while there is a diversity of opinion and many difficult and different lived experiences, it is important that we can still articulate a commitment to holy living, and to helping one another grapple with what that might mean from a biblical perspective.

Amid these instructions to take off and put on, Paul also adds in verse 23 that we should *be being* made new in our attitudes, *always putting on* our new self. Using a present continuous tense here, Paul indicates this is not a one-time re-dressing, but rather a continual process of inward renewal. We need to keep on keeping on as disciples of Jesus! With the Holy Spirit's help, we can continually take off what no longer belongs to us and put on a character that is fitting or worthy of our calling. Our old garments – old ways of thinking, scruffy habits and lies we've believed for years – need to go, and we regularly need to declutter our souls to make sure they don't creep back in. These rags no longer belong in our wardrobe and we shouldn't make room for them again.

In reality, getting rid of old mindsets or attitudes is not easy, and we might inadvertently pick up those familiar and comfortable old clothes if we are not careful. So we may choose to be truthful, most of the time. We seek to bring reconciliation, apart from in *that* situation. We work honestly, but also bend the rules here and there. We speak positively of people to their faces, but behind their backs it is a different story. How much of God's kingdom, his presence, his power do you think we miss out on because we have not taken off what we should and put on what we should?

None of us are perfect and we all make mistakes; living counter-culturally was not easy for the Ephesians and it isn't for us either. But the battle for our mind, our character and our integrity is real, and the kingdom of darkness and the kingdom of light are clearly at odds with one another. Thankfully, God is always gracious and forgiving. As we ask for his help, we can renew our minds once more and throw off our old life and the conduct that belonged there and put on the character of Christ in its place again.

The armour of God

In Ephesians 6 we encounter a second set of clothes, the armour of God. Now, to be clear, this is not an alternative set of clothes that we are called to dress in; it is not that the gentle, touchy-feely people choose the truthful and loving, cardigan-wearing outfit, while the more gritty, feisty people choose the armour option. Not at all! We are all called to wear both sets of clothes, because each set of clothes prepares us for a different battleground.

While we must fight the internal battles for our mind, character and choices, there are plenty of external battles that can lead us away from intimacy with God. As Christians, we must remember that there is always more going on behind the scenes than we see or understand. Just as there is a visible physical world, there is an invisible spiritual world. Just as there is a God who is for us, there is an opposition, an enemy of our souls, who is against us.

In the cultic and mystical culture Paul was writing in, speaking about spiritual principalities and spirits and powers would have been totally accepted. Therefore, he does not add more specific information about these powers here but teaches instead about how to overcome them. We may be less accustomed to thinking in these terms, but our experience tells us that just as God's kingdom of light is hallmarked by unity, harmony, purity and diversity, these areas will inevitably be challenged by the kingdom of darkness. We therefore need to be prepared, to be dressed appropriately and prayerfully in God's armour. Stott puts it well, saying, 'The peace which God has made through Christ's cross is to be experienced only in the midst of a relentless struggle against evil. And for this the strength of the Lord and the armour of God are indispensable.'[6]

Priscilla Shirer, in her excellent book on the armour of God, says we often make one of two mistakes when considering the spiritual realm, especially the existence of Satan:

1 'We overestimate his impact in our lives, living with an inflated, erroneous perspective of his actual influence and abilities. As a result, we are laden with undue fear and anxiety.

2 We underestimate him and miscalculate the impact of his influence in our lives. We prioritise what we can see over what we can't.'[7] The more we focus on fixing ourselves, disregarding the spiritual world, the happier the enemy of our soul will be.

Having been in church leadership, serving across many denominations for decades, we certainly recognise these two different emphases. Excuse the obvious hyperbole here, but at one end of the church spectrum it can seem as though the devil is responsible for *everything* – every bad choice, every diagnosis and every unfortunate circumstance. Times of prayer therefore emphasise curses and generational bondage, and the devil is given a great deal of focus and credit. At the other end of the spectrum, however, in some churches it feels as though any mention of 'him downstairs', or the presence of evil, seems a little unsavoury or impolite. Not very British, is it? The devil is best imagined in cartoon form with a red pointy tail, and the influence of evil in our world may be largely ignored or explained away. You get the point.

Jesus, however, while describing himself as the Good Shepherd in John 10:10–11, describes Satan as a thief, saying, 'The thief comes only to steal and kill and destroy; I have come that they may have life, and have it to the full.' There is power at work that wants to disrupt the abundant fullness of life Christ has won for you. This thief will convince you that your greatest strengths are not worth deploying and will whisper to you that your greatest weaknesses disqualify you from serving or even from being of value. He will scheme against strong Christian families and united churches, and the last thing he wants is prayerful, spiritually replenished Christians representing Christ in their workplaces and communities. He will ensure our prayer and worship are interrupted or contested (in fact, worship is frequently a battle zone in many churches), and every temptation will be thrown in the way of holy living.

Some theologians also suggest that these powers and principalities manifest themselves in unjust systems, institutions or economic or political structures, or reveal themselves in prejudice or hatred. And indeed, all forms of power can be used for harm or for good and when we idolise corporations or reward and bend our knee to unaccountable systems, it is quite possible to see why some might be considered an ungodly or even evil influence in our culture.[8] Without deifying or demonising everything, we can certainly attest that there is evil at work in the world. We might not live in Ephesus with a temple dedicated to a mythical goddess, but we are surrounded by plenty of shrines to materialism, consumerism and self-gratification that lure us to worship anything but the one true God. These are powerful forces.

The battle is in full swing, then, but the Bible reassures us that evil has not won the victory over our lives. In fact, it tells us that the devil has been:

- disarmed and humiliated (Colossians 2:15);
- overruled (Ephesians 1:20–22);
- humbled and mastered (Philippians 2:9–11);

- rendered powerless (Hebrews 2:14); and
- his hard work has been destroyed (1 John 3:8).[9]

Jesus has won victory over the kingdom of darkness and evil, which is why Paul (reiterating the underlying 'you've received it, so now live it' theme of Ephesians again) tells us we have already been given spiritual resources and authority against these powers and principalities – we therefore need to utilise them. This is excellent news for us. We already own the armour of God; we therefore need to wear it, so that we can stand firm against the tactics and schemes of the devil (Ephesians 6:11).

> Finally, be strong in the Lord and in his mighty power. Put on the full armour of God, so that you can take your stand against the devil's schemes. For our struggle is not against flesh and blood, but against the rulers, against the authorities, against the powers of this dark world and against the spiritual forces of evil in the heavenly realms. Therefore put on the full armour of God, so that when the day of evil comes, you may be able to stand your ground, and after you have done everything, to stand. Stand firm then, with the belt of truth buckled around your waist, with the breastplate of righteousness in place, and with your feet fitted with the readiness that comes from the gospel of peace. In addition to all this, take up the shield of faith, with which you can extinguish all the flaming arrows of the evil one. Take the helmet of salvation and the sword of the Spirit, which is the word of God.
> (Ephesians 6:10–17)

As we read these great words written by Paul, it is important to remember that he didn't have to work too hard to imagine a soldier, as he was writing in chains, under a Roman guard. This guard may not have been wearing the 'full' or 'complete' battle armour that this passage describes, but it seems likely he may have provided inspiration for Paul as he faced his own battles. It is also worth noting that Paul was writing to the Church and not just to people individually. Yes, we have our own personal battles, but we *all* need to be strong *together*.

With that in mind, we are once again called to intentionally and purposefully *put on* the full armour of God. This is the same language as used in Ephesians 4. And it is the *full* armour of God that Paul repeatedly recommends to us (6:11 and again in 6:13). We are not to casually throw on half a suit of armour for our battles and struggles. Just as it wouldn't work to go out for a walk on a rainy day with a decent anorak but flimsy flip-flops, so we need to be fully equipped for the storms of life that put our faith under pressure. Perhaps we sometimes miss out on the fullness of life Jesus promises because we are not fully dressed for the occasion!

So, what are we to wear?

The belt of truth (v. 14)

The belt of a soldier probably held his tunic together and his sword securely in place. This belt gives us confidence in the saving truth of Jesus, which holds us securely in place and equips us to live truthfully, with integrity, always bringing the truth into the light. When we resort to hypocrisy or deceit we play by the enemy's rules, and we certainly cannot beat the devil at his own game.

The breastplate of righteousness (v. 14)

We are made righteous because of Jesus, but this then means living righteously as a result. The breastplate is a life-or-death piece of armour; without it, one stab could cause a fatal injury. Our spiritual breastplate will guard and protect our heart and our life as we live in right relationship with God and others.

Gospel shoes (v. 15)

Our feet are fitted with readiness, and we have a firm foothold when we have peace with God. It is certainly true that having peace that passes all understanding (see Philippians 4:7) is a gift from God, and we should be ready and prepared to go out and share the good news of this peace with others.

The shield of faith (v. 16)

The word used here suggests a long oblong shield that covered the entire body. It was constructed from two layers of wood glued together and covered with linen and then hide, and was designed to put out adversaries' fiery darts or arrows dipped in pitch and set alight. We will all face fiery darts of accusation, unfair treatment, lies, ridicule, temptation, fear or even persecution. Thankfully, we have a refuge in God, and our shield of faith can extinguish those darts.

The helmet of salvation (v. 17)

This sturdy and impenetrable helmet protects our thinking and reminds us that we are saved by grace through faith. We must do whatever we can to protect our thinking – memorise Scripture, write a gratitude journal, text encouragement between friends, read or listen to great Christian books or podcasts, and guard what else we fill our brains with. It is security in our salvation that means we can hold our head up high with confidence.

The sword of the Spirit (v. 17)

Unlike all the other items, a sword can be used for both attack and defence. The sword referred to in this passage is a short sword used in close-contact battle, which makes sense as sometimes our battles are up close and personal. The Bible is both our defence and our weapon, and just as Jesus knew the Scriptures and deployed them against the devil in the wilderness, so we too can be sure of the

Spirit's power in the Bible when we are gripped by temptation, guilt or fear. It is sharper than any two-edged sword and can neutralise enemy lies. Likewise, when we are preaching or sharing the gospel, Scripture has the power to cut right through to the heart of the matter.[10]

Prayer – the ultimate armour

Many people think there are only six pieces of armour, but in fact it seems there are seven. Prayer is the final element, and it holds all the armour together. Shirer suggests, 'It is what activates all the other pieces and fortifies you as a soldier in battle. It is the device that empowers and "charges up" every other piece so they can be used effectively against the enemy.'[11] Prayer ensures our armour is Spirit-infused and enables us to face our daily battles with confidence in the Lord's strength rather than ours!

And this is why Paul ends his armour description by encouraging the believers to 'pray in the Spirit on all occasions with all kinds of prayers and requests. With this in mind, be alert and always keep on praying for all the Lord's people' (6:18). He is reinforcing something we already know but need to be constantly reminded of: prayer is not just important; it is vital. And according to these sentences it is also constant, fervent and unselfish.[12] Whereas Paul says to pray on all occasions all kinds of prayers for all people, most of us (if we are honest) pray sometimes, with some prayers, with some perseverance, for some people! But prayer enables us to encounter the presence and power of God. The way we stand against the evil one requires more than just having the right clothes on; It is about ensuring we are intimately connected with the living God who has provided them. And praying in the Spirit is praying in line, in rhythm and in conjunction with the Holy Spirit, who (it says in Romans 8:26) is interceding for us with groans that words cannot express.

Most of us, if we were asked how confident we feel about prayer, would look a little shifty. Probably few of us feel we pray enough. The truth is, prayer is not about being good enough, otherwise none of us (including everybody in the Bible besides Jesus) would be able to pray. Praying in the Spirit is not about confidence in ourselves at all. As Hebrews 4:16 reminds us, it is because of our sinless Saviour Jesus that we can 'approach God's throne of grace with confidence, so that we may receive mercy and find grace to help us in our time of need'.

Do you ever need to receive mercy?

Do you need grace in your time of need?

Do you need power and peace in the battles you face each day?

We all do.

I (Mark) remember a battle of doubt I used to fight regularly. My journey of faith doesn't have a specific decision point, as I was brought up being taught about Jesus and as far back as I can remember I simply accepted, believed and followed him. But this led to a lurking problem in my mind. Because I couldn't give an exact date of conversion when I decided to follow Jesus, I kept asking, 'Am I *really* a child of God?' I knew the truth in my mind, and held on to it, but the doubt stubbornly lingered. So on one occasion I was utterly open and honest in prayer with God, pouring out my doubt and my desire to know him more. And on that occasion, God's response was overwhelming. I clearly sensed a loving Father touching my heart and reassuring me, saying, 'I understand. I love you. You are mine.' God's presence seemed to reverberate around my soul, and his promise strengthened me and helped me to stand against the lies and doubts of the evil one.

Your story might be different, but the Bible is clear: God loves you, God wants to hear from you and God is not too busy to spend time with you. He wants you to know his continuing love, acceptance, joy, forgiveness and presence, and that is found through prayer. You can share your thoughts, feelings, fears, hopes and dreams and your entire life with a heavenly Father who will not and cannot ever let you down.

Prayer might not always be an emotional encounter, but it is vital as we seek to follow Jesus each day. And isn't it great that Paul suggests 'all kinds of prayers'? God is a *creator* God and we are creative people made in his image. There is not one set prayer format or ritual, a holy phrase or an anointed prayer that opens the floodgates of heaven. We might pray as we worship with others, or alone at home, or as we go into a meeting. As we read about Joshua, Solomon, David, Hannah, Mary and of course Jesus (and so many more in the Bible) we see different personalities praying in different circumstances with different needs. Prayer prompted sea-parting, storm-stilling, fire-sending, sick-healing, food-providing, winemaking, earth-quaking, water-walking, chain-breaking and enemy-conquering! God consistently responds when his people pray.

And prayer within the context of battles is not without precedent. For example, in Exodus 17:8–13, when the Israelites are attacked by the Amalekites, Moses tells Joshua, the leader of the Israelite army, to assemble his army and fight, while he (Moses) stands on a hill overlooking the battle, hands lifted in prayer. The battle starts and while Moses prays, the Israelites are successful. But, as time passes, Moses tires and he drops his arms. And as his arms drop, the battle turns against the Israelites, and they begin to lose. But in a beautiful example of solidarity, Aaron and Hur step in to support Moses' arms until the battle is won.

We need one another if we want to win our battles. Together we can hold the line in prayer, when alone we might wobble. When we begin to doubt or to wonder why our prayers are not always answered as we would like, others can help us to keep our eyes fixed on Jesus, who is always good, even when life is hard. Perhaps there are days when we wonder *why* we pray at all – if God knows everything anyway, what is the point? This is when we need to be honest and persist faithfully, with the support of others.

So praying on all occasions is not about trying to twist God's arm to make him respond or to convince him to see things our way. It is not muttering the Lord's Prayer under our breath throughout the day (although the Lord's Prayer as a model for prayer is not a bad place to start, as Jesus suggested it). When we pray, we are open to what God's thoughts or priorities might be, what his wisdom suggests or what courage or peace he might offer. We can punctuate our day with prayers, perhaps when we boil the kettle or walk the dog, or when we begin and end the day in bed. Praying in the Spirit on all occasions with all kinds of prayers is understanding that as children of God we can keep an open dialogue with God, inviting him into the highs and lows of each day.

Why then do we not pray regularly, or forget to pray until we are in the midst of a crisis? Perhaps our prayer life more resembles those times when we find ourselves saying to people, 'We *must* catch up soon – let's put something in the diary!' Even when it's people we really, *really* want to meet with, we can find that it rarely actually happens.

Life is complicated and it is far too easy to induce guilt over prayer. Often our days are congested, and we struggle to find the margin we need or the healthy rhythms we know would enable us to flourish in our relationships with God and with others. Sometimes our life balance does need some reflection and recalibration.[13] There are also times when we have become invested in the wrong battles entirely or we are just stressed in the extreme. Or maybe we are in the midst of a deadline season, or we have caring responsibilities or health issues that fill our spiritual, emotional and practical bandwidth. God knows the pressures we face. But praying is not supposed to be a burden or another thing on our to-do list to get around to. It is, once again, about living in the fullness of our calling that we have been created for. Just as we don't have to remember to breathe, we can learn to practise the presence of God in the ordinary and the mundane, as well as in the challenges and opportunities we encounter.

In this vein, we remember that Jesus prayed in John 15 that his disciples would 'abide' or 'remain' in him, and he in them. Prayer is not about checking in with Jesus every now and then, and our armour is not something to put on in emergencies. Our faith should be immersive and integrated into who we are. Our spiritual formation process as Christians is about walking with Jesus, living more fully in his presence and understanding the peace and authority that his presence promises.

So, whether we are serving in a food bank, looking after young children, working in an office or a hospital, getting our shopping at the supermarket or having a significant conversation with a young person, we need to be properly attired, spiritually speaking. We will never, in ourselves, have the resources we need to serve and love well. We will never summon up the wisdom, patience, faithfulness, courage, steadfastness and integrity that Jesus modelled, without the Holy Spirit's infilling. We need his presence and his power, as the armour clearly demonstrates.

In summary, our faith is something we should wear naturally and continually. It is not just an outfit for special occasions. Let's not therefore go into battle unarmed or deluded about the opposition we face. We need to keep taking off what doesn't belong to us and putting on instead what God has provided for us. What a marvellous thing it is that we can be 'strong in the Lord and in his mighty power' (Ephesians 6:10). Surely that's worth being properly dressed for.

Dress up – working it out

Reflect

Spend some time in prayer and consider what you might need to take off and put on. Which of these are easier or harder for you?

- Take off falsehood/Put on truth (4:25)
- Take off anger/Put on righteousness (4:26–27)
- Take off stealing/Put on contributing (4:28)
- Take off unwholesome talk/Put on edifying words (4:29–30)
- Take off bitterness/Put on compassion (4:31 – 5:2)
- Take off impurity/Put on thankfulness (5:3–4)

How can you intentionally respond and go deeper in your faith so that your outfit fits who you are in Christ? Is there somebody you could share or learn more with?

Recalibrate

What are the main situations in your life that feel like a battle right now?

How can you learn to actively put on the armour of God to help you in that battle? Write one example for each part of the armour in Ephesians 6.

- The belt of truth (v. 14)
- The breastplate of righteousness (v. 14)
- Gospel shoes (v. 15)
- The shield of faith (v. 16)
- The helmet of salvation (v. 17)
- The sword of the Spirit (v. 17)
- Praying in the Spirit on all occasions, with all kinds of prayers and requests (v. 18)

What about praying in the Spirit on all occasions? In his excellent book *How to Pray*,[14] Pete Greig suggests a model of prayer that helps us to PRAY regularly. Consider areas of your life where you need to look up and know more of God's power and love. Ideally, try building this cycle of prayer into your daily/regular rhythm, even if it's just for a few minutes:[15]

- *Pause* – Be still and know that God is God. Be present and focus your distracted heart and mind on Jesus.
- *Rejoice and reflect* – Linger, as Paul did, on who God is and his majesty and goodness. Worship with music or a psalm. Reflect on a verse or section of Scripture.
- *Ask* – Come before God with your desires, needs, doubts, long-ings and wider intercession for the world. Ask for his will to be done in all things.
- *Yield* – Surrender to God again, confessing any sin and emptying yourself so that you may again be filled to the measure of all the fullness of God.

Rejoice

Lord Jesus,

Thank you for equipping me with everything I need to face my battles every day. I pray that I would abide in you, as without you my battle efforts are futile. Thank you that I can dress appropriately today with your powerful armour from heaven. I agree again with your promise that no weapon formed against me shall prosper [Isaiah 54:17], and I commit to taking off what I no longer need to be wearing, and instead putting on all that is fitting for who you have called me to be.

In Jesus' mighty name. Amen.

Further reading/extra resources

https://www.practicingtheway.org/ Resources on the website and social media, with John Mark Comer encouraging churches and small groups to engage with spiritual disciplines and spiritual formation.

Amy Boucher Pye, *7 Ways to Pray* (London: SPCK, 2021). Gives excellent ideas on how to pray in all kinds of ways in all kinds of seasons.

Richard Foster, *Celebration of Discipline* (London: Hodder & Stoughton, 2008). A classic book on spiritual disciplines, rhythms and practices that help us to keep focused on Jesus.

Brother Lawrence, *The Practice of the Presence of God*. This classic book provides excellent insight into how we might learn to commune with God in the mundane and the ordinary every day.

Priscilla Shirer, *The Armor of God* (Nashville, TN: Lifeway Press, 2022), or her talk on the subject from TBN, available at: https://youtu.be/CazArZlwePM (accessed 8 November 2023).

4

Stand up

Your position and your posture matter

It has been a big year in the Madavan household as we passed the thirty-year marriage milestone. Thirty years. Obviously we were outrageously young when we tied the knot! Somebody once told us you should always celebrate anniversaries more than birthdays, because to have a birthday you just need to not die, but to have an anniversary you need to not kill anyone!

Humour aside, a lot has happened as we have travelled three decades together, in many ways against the odds, having coped with multiple house moves, various disappointments, a degenerative eye condition (Mark) and many stressful seasons. We've also experienced all kinds of blessings, including raising two wonderful daughters and building some incredible friendships, with various homes having been renovated along the way. We had no idea what we were getting ourselves into when we walked down the aisle and signed a piece of paper to say we were legally married. But learning to live in that marriage, standing firm when we wobbled, keeping going when it involved significant sacrifice... that is when a contract became a marriage.

Of course, not everyone reading this book is married and not all marriages last for thirty years for all kinds of reasons; we have been fortunate in many ways. But be it a marriage, a friendship or any long-term relationship, it is one thing to connect and commit, and then another thing altogether to spend a lifetime continually connecting and committing, and coming through the testing times that will inevitably come our way. And church is no different, is it? We are just a bunch of people who commit to each other and then proceed to rub each other up the wrong way from time to time! We are united in our faith, but it is a decision to love, to forgive, to overcome the hurdles and to keep going. The Church is far from perfect and can be painful and disappointing at times, but here we are, at the 2,000-year-ish milestone, and the Church is still standing, building, adapting, sharing and demonstrating God's love in communities around the world. Quite an achievement.

Not only is the Church still standing, however, but we are also still standing up for Jesus and the love, mercy, justice and compassion that Jesus represents. The Church is not called to step down, sit down or pipe down; we are called to stand up![1] We are the people of God on a mission, living with a purpose, with a gospel of good news to share and to embody wherever we find ourselves. This doesn't mean that standing up will involve being aggressive or combative, constantly declaring war against every issue, but standing up for Jesus and stepping out for him may well be costly at times. We don't stand alone, however; we stand in God's strength, committed to living out the calling we have received and the promises we made. For better and for worse, we need to stand firm and stand together.

Stand firm

Some years ago, we went away for a few days, leaving our daughters to fend for themselves. It was the first time we had left them, and we were travelling a fair distance to Scotland to stay with some friends and speak at their church, so it was not going to be possible to quickly pop back if problems arose. As good (and ever-so-slightly paranoid) parents, we obviously left sufficient food, gave them multiple contact numbers in case of emergencies, set explicit rules about the lack of parties expected, and went on our merry way. What could possibly go wrong? Quite a lot, it turned out.

On the evening of the first day, we received a panicked phone call informing us that the garage, which was stacked full of stuff, was completely flooded, and they had no idea where the water was coming from. It wasn't the washing machine, it wasn't the boiler and it wasn't the roof, but it was definitely flooding, and the water was rising. It had been raining hard, but they could not see where the water was getting in. Being over 400 miles away, our only advice was to lift everything they could from the floor, sweep water like mad and wait for us to get home. When we returned, Mark put on his flood-investigator hat and was duly baffled. But when it started raining again, the problem was immediately clear. A drainpipe that emptied into a soakaway drain outside the garage was blocked and therefore not draining at all but overflowing instead. Cue many hours of digging out a silted-up drain and many months of running outside whenever it rained!

Just as our house had a vulnerability, so we need to be aware that we all have weak spots. We all have overlooked points of entry in our attitudes and actions where the enemy can get a foothold and cause damage, disappointment or disunity. It could be that there are some habits we haven't been vigilant about or an issue we've not wanted to examine too closely. Perhaps we are just busy, tired and distracted, and possibly our spiritual maintenance programme isn't what it should be! No wonder Paul, coming towards the end of his letter, writes so clearly about standing firm. Indeed, the whole thrust of the section on the armour of God (written just after the paragraphs about mutual submission) emphasises the importance of being able to stand firm. In one passage in Ephesians 6, the believers are told to stand, stand firm, stand their ground and, after they have done everything, stand. Paul is definitely making a point!

The last thing Paul wanted was for his fellow believers to lose the ground they had been given or to compromise on what they now knew. He longed for them to stay united, and since they had been given a new status, a new life and a new community in Christ, he longed for them to guard it well and 'take [their] stand against the devil's schemes' (v. 11). Note that he didn't suggest they apathetically hang in there and hope for the best. No, this call to *stand* is a positive military term meaning to 'hold your ground' or 'maintain your position'. We are called to be strong in the Lord and in his mighty power, with his resources enabling us to hold our ground. Don't forget that we have been blessed in the heavenly realms with every spiritual blessing in Christ. We have been chosen, adopted, redeemed, forgiven and given God's wisdom, and we have the Holy Spirit as a deposit and guarantee (Ephesians 1:3–14). This is a strong position. We have been given everything we need to stand firm with confidence, and therefore we need to do so.

Standing our ground or holding our position as Christians isn't about being aggressive or stubborn, refusing to give way or to learn from others. Neither is standing firm about standing in the way of progress, arms folded at the very idea of change. Rather, standing firm is about deploying our faith and being consistently confident in who and whose we are. We cannot possibly advance or take any new ground God has planned for us while we are in danger of retreating or at risk of being pulled away from our faith. The ground we have been given is sacred. It has been hard-won. We are new creations and new citizens together, all made possible by Jesus. We have been given a new purpose and new way of thinking, and a new family. But none of these things are uncontested or easy to maintain. So we need to stand firm.

You see, it is possible to have won a war but still need to defend your territory. Historians tell us that the D-Day landings on 6 June 1944 were a pivotal moment in the Second World War. In many ways, victory was won at this point, even though on the front lines, the enemy was still fighting. In a similar way, we know with Jesus the victory over our enemy and death and evil is won. It is finished!

However, the enemy is still fighting, and we all have vulnerable front lines that we need to defend against attack so that we can also advance and build God's kingdom together.

It is good to be as self-aware and honest as possible about our vulnerabilities. It is not a weakness but a strength to admit we all have our own shadow side, hidden issues and backstage areas that are less than shiny. None of us are quite as fabulous as our Instagram and Facebook posts suggest. In many cases, the battles we face are actually won behind the scenes when nobody is watching,[2] so it is good to be honest about the fact that we all have challenges, because as we share our vulnerabilities, we give permission and courage to others to do the same. Isolation and the belief that we are the only one to struggle in a certain area is a huge factor in whether we can fight our battles effectively. *None* of us are above temptation, mistakes, self-doubt or sinful behaviour, so let's not pretend we are immune. While we will not all struggle with the same things, we need to be courageous and bring issues into the light where we need help. It is then that others can help us to maintain our defences and stand our ground. And it is also then that we rediscover the grace of God, which never lets us go.

So where are your silted-up drains, as it were? Where might God be asking you to intentionally defend and protect a vulnerable area or some ground you've been given? Here are some ideas for starters:

Words

For some of us, an area of risk is our words. Maybe we find it easy to bend the truth to fit our purposes, or we justify our lack of truth-telling by saying it is for the benefit of others. Perhaps we know we can jump to criticise with spoken or written words, using our phone or our screen to speak unkindly. Maybe we subconsciously participate in gossip or the sharing of information, which brings disunity. In the New Testament book of James, in chapter 3, James tells us that despite the tongue being a small part of our body, like a tiny spark it has the power to start a forest fire. For me (Mark) I know that when I am tired this can become a vulnerable area, where humour or speaking directly (which are often strengths) can fall into sarcasm or over-directness. I need to stand firm and not give the enemy a foothold, because words are powerful.

Thoughts

As has already been said, our thinking matters, because our thoughts become our habits and our habits are the building blocks of life. Perhaps that is why Paul says in another letter: 'whatever is true, whatever is noble, whatever is right, whatever is pure, whatever is lovely, whatever is admirable – if anything is excellent or praiseworthy – think about such things' (Philippians 4:8). None of us want resentment, bitterness, jealousy, cynicism or fear to take root, and it can help to choose instead to focus on whatever is pure and admirable. So when Paul tells the Ephesians not to let the sun go down on their anger (4:26), it is because when we allow our negative emotions and thinking to fester, it can so easily escalate and separate us from one another and God.

Of course, that is not to suggest we can simply suppress, overlook or deny our emotions or difficulties. For us, when it comes to Mark's sight loss, for example, no amount of positive thinking can change how hard it is to go blind, and there have been many difficult days. But even then, it is true that we can choose to focus on the many things he *can* do and not just on what he *can't* do. We can remember how God has faithfully helped and provided for us thus far. The issues will be different for everyone, but we live in an uncertain world with so much fear and anxiety about so many things, and for those struggling with depression or other mental health issues, this can be a far greater challenge. It is not always possible to just think happy thoughts or look on the bright side. But this is not what Paul is saying.

For all of us, where we default to patterns of faulty thinking or keep getting stuck playing the same mental record repeatedly, the Bible, modern science and therapeutic techniques tell us we can indeed 'renew our thinking'.[3] While some of us will need to get the right professional advice and support, every one of us has a thought life to nurture and protect. We should be encouraged that daily habits of prayer, memorising Scripture, being thankful for what is good and repeating promises of God can be powerful and reassuring – not just affecting our emotional well-being, but growing our faith in every circumstance, whatever our feelings and struggles might be.[4]

Actions

I (Cathy) distinctly remember watching our children, when they were toddlers, trying to work out what they could get away with. My daughter knew she was not allowed to put bread in the video player (remember video players?!), but she would walk towards it with her sandwich, looking over her shoulder at me to see just how serious I was about this rule. Feeding the machine was fun, after all! We may not be toddlers, but we probably wonder whether we can get away with stuff from time to time, be that nudging above the speed limit, looking at something we know we shouldn't online or spending money we know we don't have (to name three examples of any possible number). We may not be brawling on the streets, drinking recklessly or committing fraud, so we tell ourselves that we are OK.[5] But are we? It is incredibly important we don't get accustomed to or blasé about flirting with danger. It makes sense to decide on some clear and pre-emptive guard rails or boundaries that limit our exposure to temptation before we get too close to the edge. It's good to back away from the precipice! If we know there is some slippery ground where we are likely not to stand firm, we need to stand back from it wherever possible, and we may need support and accountability to stand firm on more solid ground.

Standing firm each day is not easy. And whenever we seek to align ourselves with Jesus, it is likely to be contested. We can certainly testify that at times when we have made a decision to stand firm or step up for Jesus, life has sometimes become more difficult, not less. Perhaps we doubt our decision or begin to feel a bit silly or embarrassed, we get let down by others, or we wonder whether it is worth it or whether we did the right thing. The enemy knows exactly what tactics to deploy. And while not every bad thing that happens in life is a spiritual attack (tough stuff does just happen), we are told to wear our spiritual armour for a reason and to keep standing firm, with support from others.

Stand humbly

Standing firm and standing up for Jesus might sound strong and heroic, but in reality most of us don't feel like superheroes. Of course, it would be great to have a few superpowers. Cathy is a fan of Wonder Woman. She wouldn't mind getting her hands on her own 'lasso of truth' that compels anyone to tell and understand the truth. After much contemplation I think I (Mark) would choose Superman. He can fly, and who wouldn't want to fly? He is super-strong, super-bulletproof, super-fast, with super-hearing and various other super-attributes. And our favourite superheroes also usually stand up for good, stand up for others and certainly stand up in extraordinary outfits! But we are not superheroes, and even if we were, being able to dominate, eliminate or manipulate others into defeat is not ever our goal. We are not to use power, strength or any supernatural gift we have been given to be superior, to control or to impress others. Far from it.

We are, in fact, called to something entirely different: humility and submission. Now these attributes might not sound as exciting as a truth lasso or the ability to fly, but in the kingdom of God, they are powerful. Humility and submission can disarm disagreements, empower others and release the presence of God into relationships. The dictionary defines submission as surrender or giving in to others, but the Bible illuminates this further, describing submission as our willing surrender to God and the freedom to give sacrificially to others. Ultimately, in the upside-down – or right-side-up – kingdom of God, values that the world might consider to be meeker or weaker demonstrate that God is far kinder and stronger than any human (or superhero) could ever be.

Written in the 1400s, Thomas à Kempis' book *The Imitation of Christ* is probably the most widely read Christian book outside the Bible. His writings have influenced many others, including St Augustine. In his second chapter he addresses the call to think humbly of oneself:

> If it seemeth to thee that thou knowest many things, and understandest them well, know also that there are many more things which thou knowest not. Be not high-minded, but rather confess thy ignorance. Why desirest thou to lift thyself above another, when there are found many more learnèd and more skilled in Scripture than thou? ... To account nothing of oneself, and to think always kindly and highly of others, this is great and perfect wisdom.[6]

While the translated words may seem old-fashioned, the sentiment feels as relevant as ever. We so often want to look as if we know more than we do, or we elevate ourselves and our opinions and diminish others in the process, even in casual conversation (a sign of insecurity rather than security). Our words often show that we are competing and comparing rather than thinking highly of others. But in Colossians 3:12 and 1 Peter 5:5 we are told to clothe ourselves in humility, and the theme continues in Ephesians. Less about me; more about you. Adopting a posture of humility, I am then also able to submit or surrender myself to others.

Obviously, we need to insert some caveats here swiftly, to avoid any misunderstanding. As soon as the word 'submission' is uttered, we must accept that this concept has often been used against people rather than for them. Especially as we turn to some of the texts in Ephesians concerning husbands and wives, slaves and masters, parents and children, we need to remember that the Bible is not a weapon to wield but the word of God that brings freedom and life. Where there are disproportionate or unequal power dynamics at play, it is all too easy for God's principles to be upended, twisted or even turned into something toxic. We have all seen power used badly in relationships, politics and business, and very sadly also in churches.

But how we stand does make a difference, and a posture of humility is one that willingly lays aside our desires, our wants and even our rights to serve God and others where we are called to do so. Submission towards one another therefore is a choice, where we freely and sacrificially give to others as a sign of our surrender to God. This posture is good news to those around us – when we are secure enough to deal with others without arrogance or self-righteousness, when we are teachable and able to empower those around us, we foster trust and a context of mutual respect, safety and care.

However, one of the many problems we find as we approach humility or submission (which are distinct but closely linked) is that in our broken humanity and our individualistic culture, we are less interested in humbling ourselves and more interested in success, power, protecting our rights and maintaining our comfort. While the world continually tells us that getting exactly what you want is the way to happiness, biblically speaking it is humility and submission that are well-worn pathways towards fruitfulness and fulfilment. Moreover, increasingly we see a conflation of things we think are our rights and things that are actually our likes, and we don't want to compromise on any of the things we like! Now, obviously, human rights should be protected and championed, and those who have been oppressed or exploited deserve to be heard and fully recognised. But not everything is our right. Over the years, we have met folk who think it is their right to get the promotion, to be chosen for the team, to have amazing kids' work every Sunday and to be involved in every decision. We might *like* these things, we might even *deserve* them, but they are not our right and it is not always possible or desirable to have everything we want, when we want it.

Biblical submission, then, is primarily modelled in Jesus. In Philippians 2:1–11, we read a beautiful and moving account of Jesus Christ's humility – the high King of heaven making himself nothing, humbled and obedient to death, even death on a cross, which was the ultimate humiliation. This is our Saviour. Jesus had all the power of heaven at his disposal but relinquished it for us. So, as we follow Jesus, we choose a posture that emulates his servant-heartedness. Let's remember that while Jesus was at his most vulnerable, with the horror of the crucifixion before him, he expressed three times from the depths of his heart his desire not to have to endure the cross if at all possible. The suffering ahead of him was unimaginable, but in that moment he said, 'My Father, if it is not possible for this cup to be taken away unless I drink it, may your will be done' (Matthew 26:42). It was this act of submission from the King of kings that won us freedom, forgiveness and restoration in our relationship with God.

As apprentices to Jesus, therefore, this is also part of our calling. In Matthew 16:24, Mark 8:34 and Luke 9:23 Jesus talks about denying ourselves, surrendering and taking up our cross daily if we want to follow him. Deny ourselves? Pick up a cross? Surrender ourselves? That doesn't sound easy. Does this mean abandoning our emotional well-being, burning ourselves out or ignoring the desires of our hearts?

Let's remember it was the same Jesus who said, 'Come to me, all you who are weary and burdened, and I will give you rest. Take my yoke upon you and learn from me, for I am gentle and humble in heart, and you will find rest for your souls. For my yoke is easy and my burden is light' (Matthew 11:28–30). Jesus is kind. He does not want to punish us or limit the life he promised we would live in all its fullness through him. But there *is* a cost to learning to follow Jesus, and it does involve sacrifice. Wonderfully, however, as we lay down the yoke of the world, with all its performance pressure, debt-ridden excess and focus on the superficial, we discover something far purer and greater. As we learn to give, love, pray, forgive, rest in Jesus and serve others, even when it is costly we find the grace, ease and companionship of Jesus, who has walked this path before us.

Submission, at its core, is the understanding that I can choose to deny myself and my ego, which always want to promote, prioritise and protect me, myself and I. I can choose to surrender my 'right' to have everything my way or to have every question or prayer answered the way I would like. Having a humble heart means understanding there are opinions and solutions that differ from mine, and that's OK. In fact, humility and the ability to submit to others are not qualities to be mistaken for having low self-esteem or being a doormat. Jesus had total security in who he was but chose to surrender himself, nevertheless. That was a sign of strength, not weakness. We can be secure, strong, confident and content, yet choose to restrain both our strengths and our wayward desires.

We *can* choose our posture.

With our head held high, we can bow down low to relinquish some of our resources, power, preferences, time and desires in order to gain greater intimacy with God and unity with others. We can intentionally empower the people around us instead of main-taining power for ourselves. Where our culture and our natural desires shout, 'Here I am!' a Christlike character says, 'There you are!' instead. Indeed, the old adage is pretty spot on: humility is not thinking less of yourself; it is thinking of yourself less!

Stand together

In Ephesians, then, Paul applies this call to humility and mutual submission to the believers he is writing to. In chapter 5, verse 21, he summarises what he is about to explore by saying these significant words: 'Submit to one another out of reverence for Christ.' Shall we pause here for a moment of honesty? When it comes to submitting to God, at least we know that he is perfect and good and trustworthy. But when it comes to submitting to anybody else, we are probably less convinced! Especially when we are also honest about the power imbalances, systems, customs and relational issues we are aware of that make this subject so difficult. And yet here Paul encourages us, out of our reverence for Christ, to consider our position and posture in our relationships and how we might submit to one another.

First, there are verses about wives and husbands:

Wives, submit yourselves to your own husbands as you do to the Lord. For the husband is the head of the wife as Christ is the head of the church, his body, of which he is the Saviour. Now as the church submits to Christ, so also wives should submit to their husbands in everything.

Husbands, love your wives, just as Christ loved the church and gave himself up for her to make her holy, cleansing her by the washing with water through the word, and to present her to himself as a radiant church, without stain or wrinkle or any other blemish, but holy and blameless. In this same way, husbands ought to love their wives as their own bodies. He who loves his wife loves himself.
(Ephesians 5:22–28)

He then addresses parents and children:

Children, obey your parents in the Lord, for this is right. 'Honour your father and mother' – which is the first commandment with a promise – 'so that it may go well with you and that you may enjoy long life on the earth.'

Fathers, do not exasperate your children; instead, bring them up in the training and instruction of the Lord.
(Ephesians 6:1–4)

Finally Paul addresses slaves who are part of the household, and their masters:

Slaves, obey your earthly masters with respect and fear, and with sincerity of heart, just as you would obey Christ. Obey them not only to win their favour when their eye is on you, but as slaves of Christ, doing the will of God from your heart. Serve wholeheartedly, as if you were serving the Lord, not people, because you know that the Lord will reward each one for whatever good they do, whether they are slave or free.

And masters, treat your slaves in the same way. Do not threaten them, since you know that he who is both their Master and yours is in heaven, and there is no favouritism with him.
(Ephesians 6:5–9)

Who knows how many thousands of pages have been written about these verses? And we certainly cannot perform full due diligence here with regard to exegeting their full context and meaning both then and in the present. Let us, for now, be reminded that standing up for Jesus is a call to stand up for the values of Jesus we read about across Scripture. These verses come *after* Ephesians 3:7 where Paul describes himself as a 'servant of this gospel', and 3:8 where he says, 'I am less than the least of all the Lord's people.' He then says in Ephesians 4:2, 'Be completely humble and gentle; be patient, bearing with one another in love.' Paul was incredibly bold and courageous, and indeed was imprisoned for his faith. He definitely stood up for Jesus. But he also did it in humility and wanted his readers to behave similarly in their relationships.

In these early Christian congregations, then, wives, husbands, parents, children, masters and servants or slaves were all present. Paul was speaking to these Christian households where people were learning to live out their new faith in their culture together. He was explaining that whatever our age, status or position, our relationship with Jesus Christ should shape our attitude towards others. After all, we are one in Christ, together. Paul is not commenting specifically on the pros and cons of a hierarchical and patriarchal culture but does address these various people equally, which is no small thing. We know that the subjugation and exploitation of women, children, slaves and trafficked people were and are appalling injustices, and should be condemned. Where we as individuals, churches or organisations have been complicit in any unjust systems, or have perpetuated attitudes, stereotypes or prejudice, we should accept it, repent and work to humble ourselves and elevate others wherever possible.

A relevant and pertinent biblical principle here is that all people are created by God in his image and are therefore equal before God. Nobody is inferior or superior in his eyes. In fact, in Scripture we see how God often chooses and uses the least likely, the least honoured and those with least status to demonstrate his power and love. In Ephesians, Paul brings into focus this new humanity that unites us all – Jew, Gentile, man, woman, older, younger, master or slave.[7] It is in this context that we are called to submit to one another 'out of reverence for Christ' and 'as to the Lord'. As we honour Jesus, we also honour one another.

These verses, then, do not defend unlimited authority or unconditional obedience. Any power, authority or influence we have been given, no matter how limited or extensive, is never for our own selfish or self-serving reasons; it is always for the good of others and it should be mutual. Indeed, when someone misuses their power to command what God forbids or to forbid what God commands, then 'our duty is no longer conscientiously to submit, but to conscientiously refuse to do so'.[8] As one theologian once said, we must differentiate between *authority* and *tyranny*.[9] Wherever any of us have influence or power, owing to age, class, education, position, gender, beauty, fame, wealth or any other factor, we need to remember our responsibilities to those we affect. After all, most of us have power or agency of some kind, whether we are aware of it or not.

Of course, in the ancient world, attitudes were very different from those of today. As part of the Jewish morning prayer, a Jewish man would give thanks to God that he had not made him 'a Gentile, a slave or a woman'. A woman was not so much a person but a possession with no legal status or rights. Her role in marriage was subservience. It would therefore have been highly unusual for Paul to exhort a husband repeatedly (six times!) to *love* and care, and to advocate for a mutual partnership of any kind, let alone to suggest that this love would demonstrate the love of Christ for the Church. As theologian Marg Mowczko points out, it can only be a good thing if the head and the body are united and working together as one, honouring God together.[10]

In our church, we have a wonderful couple who have been married for over sixty years. Since we have clocked up a mere thirty years, less than half their time together, I (Cathy) asked them what the secret was to their successful relationship. The man, with a twinkle in his eye, told me he had learned two words that made all the difference. Eager to learn more, I asked for this hard-earned wisdom. What were these two words? He chuckled and said, 'Yes, dear!' Well, that made me laugh, but actually I love that this gentleman still wants to please his wife, and she clearly wants to please him too, after so many years together. In any good relationship the key is not 'What can I take?' but 'What can I give?' It is asking how I can support, encourage and champion you, knowing you will do the same for me. Whatever our different roles or personalities, we are called to demonstrate our love for Christ together.

In a similar vein to wives, in the ancient world children and slaves also had no legal standing whatsoever. Commentator William Barclay explains:

> A Roman father had absolute power over his family. He could sell them as slaves, he could make them work in the fields even in chains, he could punish as he liked and could even inflict the death penalty. Further, the power of the Roman father extended over the child's whole life, so long as the father lived.[11]

Clearly, modern parenting courses had not been created then! We thank God that Jesus honoured children so obviously, resetting those expectations, and that so much has changed since then. Those of us who are parents are never called to dominate but to create households of unconditional love with appropriate boundaries and support, so that our children might grow and flourish. Of course, there are never any guarantees about how children will turn out, but we can pray and love and support one another through the challenges, and serve the parents, children and youth in our churches wherever possible.[12]

Of course, it seems deeply unsettling to us that Paul then goes on to address slaves, but we must remember, as theologian N. T. Wright explains it, that 'Paul could no more envisage a world without slavery than we can envisage a world without electricity'.[13] Slaves would have been a normal part of the household, and some were treated well, while others were not. Wright suggests that if this was written today, Paul would have addressed employers and employees instead. Again, we thank God that what was once normal is now not accepted, and we must continue to pray that God would liberate those affected by the scourge of the modern-day slave trade.

So, Paul's letter to the Ephesians was not written to endorse patriarchy or oppression, coercion or manipulation. It was written to endorse selfless love and responsibility for others within a culture where this Christian message of how to treat those in your care would have been totally countercultural. And if we can look beyond the original context here, we can grasp Paul's principle that whatever our socio-economic situation, marital status or age, we too can choose our attitude and a posture of servant-heartedness. We all have influence or power over who we are, no matter what our role or rank. We all have a say over our character, and we can serve, lead, relate, work and parent with diligence and humility. And as we do, we demonstrate that we are standing as the body of Christ together.

While these verses have not always been used to bring life, freedom and unity, we should remain committed to the principle that Jesus calls us to voluntary self-submission and interdependence in a context of mutual care, respect and love. Clearly – and this is worth reiterating – we must *always* advocate and work towards fair, equitable and just systems for all, and we should support those who have been oppressed or mistreated in any way. But also, daily, wherever we are, we should be prepared to humble ourselves, to yield where necessary and to serve one another freely because we serve Jesus: I give myself up for you, as you give yourself up for me, as Christ gave himself up for us all.

Stand up for righteousness

As we have explored, *how* we stand as Christians is significant and so is standing firm and holding our ground. But there is more. We are also to stand up and make a difference in the world, positively influencing every sphere of society. We do not just have a ground to defend; we have territory to extend for Jesus! While Christianity as a religion certainly cannot claim an unblemished history around the world, it is also true that the Church has often been known as the people of Jesus who have stood up and cared for the poor, created orphan charities, welcomed refugees, fed the hungry, nursed the sick and campaigned against slavery and other social ills. Today, in villages, towns and cities across the UK and beyond, local councillors, police officers and community leaders are thankful for the Church and its work with the young, the old and those in need.

In our last church, where we served for eighteen years, we had a vision that we would be a church our community could not live without. When we arrived, the people were lovely, but our community impact was limited. Over the years, many initiatives and relationships were built, and local politicians became friends of ours as we worked together for our area. Now we have moved to the area of Fishponds in Bristol, which is a beautifully diverse community with many needs, and it is wonderful to be in a church that is already so stuck in, caring and loving, with houses set up for those at risk of homelessness and addiction, a food bank, a Ukrainian support hub, help for those integrating from Hong Kong, luncheon clubs, mentoring for women ex-offenders, multiple family activities and more. Likewise, in most towns and cities there are Christians and church congregations stepping up and standing up for those who need support in all kinds of ways.

Why do we do this? It isn't just to keep busy or to fulfil a religious duty. As the Church we are Jesus' people, and we serve and love because Jesus loved us first. We prioritise people because Jesus prioritised people. We sit and listen and value others because we too are created for fellowship and love. We share our faith because we too were once told the good news by somebody. In our families, workplaces, communities and churches, God not only calls us to hold securely to our position in Christ, but he also wants us to play our part, using our gifts and passions to take new ground for his glory.

And, of course, our calling as churches to stand up and stand firm in our faith is both wonderfully local and global. We are called to a deep sense of solidarity and unity across streams, denominations and nations. It is good to be reminded that we are a global Church with millions of local expressions of faith, and our labels and tribes matter less than our calling to be a humbly united Church that expresses God's unconditional love in a fractured world. As we stand together and speak out against oppression and injustice, and speak up for the marginalised, for the dignity of life and for godly ethics and values in life, we become witnesses together for the restoration Jesus offers and the abundant life he brings.

Of this we can be sure: as we stand up for Jesus and others, empowered by the Spirit, God will be with us. When we stand up in unity for those who are marginalised or persecuted, or we stand up for standards in public life, we release the kingdom of God into dark places. When we stand up for fairness, and when we show hospitality and compassion towards those who are overlooked, oppressed or stereotyped, we are demonstrating the love of God in action. When we stand up for the family, for faithfulness and for the freedom to express our faith, we are being ambassadors for Christ. God has given us a mandate to stand. Yes, we choose a posture of humility, but humility does not mean timidity or fear (2 Timothy 1:7). Our faith compels us to stand firm where others would withdraw, and to speak where others would remain silent. And as we draw near to God, he will surely speak to our hearts about where he wants us to stand – individually and together.

Where even now might the Holy Spirit be whispering for us to

- stand up against injustice;
- stand up for the next generation;
- stand up with those who are struggling to stand alone;
- stand our ground where we face temptation;
- stand our ground on values and principles that honour God;

- stand our ground where others would pull us away;
- stand firm in who we are in Christ;
- stand firm in the promises of God;
- stand firm in prayer and thanksgiving?

If ever there was a time to stand, it is now. This is your moment and the Church's moment to stand up. To stand your ground. To stand firm. To stand with others and for others. And then, after everything, to stay standing with the power and peace of Jesus to protect and guide you as you stand with him and for him.

And be assured, God is standing with you.

Stand up – working it out

Reflect

Take a look at the wheel below. Where would you say things are standing firm, positive and honouring to God, and where might you be more vulnerable? If outside the wheel is standing firm but inside is struggling in this area, mark where you would assess your spiritual and emotional health to be.

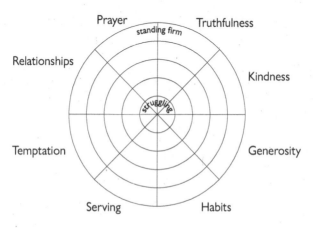

When you have finished, notice the consistency (or not!), and the areas where you might need support, prayer or an action plan. We do not need to be perfect, but we need to know how to stand firm.

Recalibrate

- Write down what you think of when you read the words 'humility' or 'submission'. Now consider how biblical mutual submission could help to foster unity and not disunity.
- List five things/people/places God has placed on your heart to stand up for.
- How will you continue to step up and stand up in God's strength?

Rejoice

Servant King Jesus,

Thank you that you chose to humble yourself for us. Fill me with your Holy Spirit again today, that I might stand in humility, serving others as you did. Help me to stand firm against the enemy's tactics, and to stand *with* others and *for* others. I surrender and yield myself to you again, so that I may honour, serve and bless others I meet today.

For your glory. Amen.

Further reading

Simon Barrington and Justin Humphreys, *Just Leadership: Putting integrity and justice at the heart of how you lead* (London: SPCK, 2021).

Gary Chapman, *The 5 Love Languages: The secret to love that lasts* (Chicago, IL: Moody Publishers, 2015).

Andy Frost and Katharine Hill, *Raising Faith: Helping our children find a faith that lasts* (Care for the Family, 2018).

Ben Lindsay, *We Need to Talk About Race: Understanding the Black experience in White Majority churches* (London: SPCK, 2019).

Lucy Peppiatt, *Rediscovering Scripture's Vision for Women: Fresh perspectives on disputed texts* (London: IVP, 2019).

5

Rise up

Your life has a purpose in Christ

Ephesians may be a short letter, but we hope you have been struck, as we have, by the riches contained within its six chapters. It is, in many ways, a handbook for living faithfully to God in unity with others. It is a mandate for Christians not only to survive but to thrive, even as we live in an environment that is hostile to our faith. But most of all, perhaps, this letter is a heartfelt response to Jesus the Messiah, whose undying love has given us new life. How marvellous it is that where once we were spiritual grave-dwellers, we are now 'up and alive'. Where once we may have felt unworthy, we now know we are chosen, adopted and called by the King of kings. Where once we might have built our lives on shaky ground, we can now stand our ground and gain new ground for Jesus' glory. We therefore willingly take off what belongs to our old life and put on characteristics and resources that flow from every spiritual blessing we have received.

Make no mistake, then, Ephesians is far more than a letter about doctrine or a missive about behaviour modification; it is concerned with transformation and nothing less. It is a Spirit-infused manual about how we live out what we believe in the power we have received. This letter should cause our hearts to rise in worship and our lives to rise again towards the purposes of God.

Rise above

In 2023 I (Cathy) was fortunate enough to travel to Uganda with Compassion on behalf of Spring Harvest. I was part of a team that would be serving at the event, and it was a special time, visiting projects, seeing the Church very much 'up and alive' in every way, worshipping wholeheartedly, serving joyfully and caring deeply for those most in need in their communities. While the challenges were clear to see, the response of the gifted and kind people serving in the Kampala region was even clearer. Their circumstances were less than ideal, but their response was to rise above their circumstances, love the poor and work tirelessly for the kingdom of God.

One day, Beatrice (one of the brilliant Spring Harvest team) and I went to visit a family in their home, where we were due to film the story of a sponsored child called Monica. As it happened, it was Monica's seventeenth birthday on the day. Since we were gate-crashing her birthday, it was decided we would take a lovely cake with her name on top, which we picked up in our off-road vehicle and held carefully as we navigated the unmade road! We arrived at the semi-rural plantation home to be greeted by Monica, her mother Divine and her brothers. We walked past the sugar canes and crops growing in the distinctive red soil to find the house. It was in bad repair, with inadequate roofing, no glass in the windows and no door in the doorway, but let me tell you, the welcome was five-star. We were warmly invited to sit and talk together around the basic wooden table where we placed the birthday cake. We opened the box and enthusiastically sang 'Happy birthday'.

And then the atmosphere changed. Monica paused, looked around the room and smiled as she regarded the cake, which was clearly a huge luxury for her. When a slice was cut and given to her, she paused again. The room became quiet as Monica took a small piece of cake in her hand, leaned over the table and with a gentle smile and a slight bow fed the cake directly into the mouth of her mother. We all sat, deeply moved, and watched her as she then continued to quietly feed the next pieces to Beatrice, me, the cameramen and the Compassion staff. She quietly and humbly elevated a moment of gratitude into something intimate, sacred and almost ceremonial. It reminded us of Jesus washing the disciples' feet, or perhaps going forward to receive Communion. Where we thought we would bless her with a cake, she in turn blessed us in a far greater way with that same cake, demonstrating the kind of poise, dignity, hospitality and generosity you don't often see in a seventeen-year-old girl. We knew we were participating in a moment none of us would ever forget, and there was not a dry eye in that room.

Let's be honest, it was not as if Monica could deny or overlook the limitations she faced; in fact, they had partly made her who she was. But she was not defined by where she lived or her challenges. Her love for Jesus was so real and her sense of who she was in Christ was so secure, she was able to rise above what you could see, to bless others with what you can't see – eternal hope. I learned a lot that day, listening to Monica talk about how she shared her faith with her neighbours and school friends, and her passion for God's word. Beatrice and I left with a deep sense of God's presence, and a reassurance that in God's kingdom it is possible to be in our circumstances but to simultaneously rise above them to be who God calls us to be.

We saw this ability to rise up again and again in Uganda. We met Richmond, a pre-eminent Christian leader in that nation, training and equipping thousands of other pastors and leaders. He was once a Compassion-sponsored child himself, having lived in harrowing circumstances in a slum. We met the adoptive mum of a tiny baby called Miracle, who had been discarded in a paper bag in a ditch, but was now being adored and cared for in a family that didn't have much other than love to give. There were so many other people whose stories were unimaginably difficult but whose joy and commitment to others were humbling to say the least.

But we don't have to travel to Uganda to know people who have had to rise above their circumstances. Closer to home, when I consider how Mark faithfully leads a church despite the frustrations and difficulties of his sight loss, I am full of admiration. We have friends who have somehow bounced back from devastating disappointments or who are living with loss or chronic illness, and their resilience is a powerful testimony. Right now, we are walking alongside precious friends who are navigating a devastating diagnosis, and yet they choose to continually bless others with hospitality and kindness. Elsewhere, another friend of ours in her seventies has just started a doctorate-level theological qualification despite what others might expect of a woman her age. Yet another friend has adopted two children with complex needs, and parents them alone (albeit with fantastic support), continually inspiring us with her resilience. Over the years, we have witnessed folk who have dreamed about starting a business or a ministry and against all the odds they have stepped out and deployed their faith. It really is possible to rise above what we can currently see, to participate in what God already sees.

It is a challenge, but maybe the reason we *don't* see God move as much as we would like is that most of us would prefer comfort to having to stretch our faith muscles too far. Naturally, we prefer to make our own (ideally risk-free) plans, which we can sustain with our own resources. But what if we gave God a little more room to manoeuvre by stepping out in faith? In our experience, it is often when we have *had* to trust God that God proves himself not only to be faithful but to exceed our expectations. It turns out that God really 'is able to do immeasurably more than all we ask or imagine, according to his power that is at work within us' (Ephesians 3:20). When we have learned that this is true, we are more likely to rise up and step out in faith again.

Maybe, like us, you sense that now is the time to rise up and step out again. It is a new season and God is always doing a new thing. Perhaps it is time to rise again in faith, despite our discomfort or past experiences. It is right to take time to lament where necessary, but there is also a time to lay down at the cross of Jesus any disappointment, loss, betrayal or confusion we may have felt, and to trust that God can resurrect, redeem and use anything for his glory. It may be that not everything has gone our way, but that is not the end of our story. We have hope, and with God's help the next chapter may well be the best one yet.

This certainly rings true as we read Ephesians. Paul was obviously not writing in his comfort zone. As we know, this letter was written by a man under armed guard, who could not do any of the things he would have chosen and planned to do. The plan A for his life that Paul had hoped for had not materialised. He could not travel, could not deliver the letter himself and could not teach in the synagogue or the public square as he would have liked. But Paul somehow rose above this and focused on what he *could* do – he could write and he could deploy his brilliant mind and his passion for God and people through his letters to those young churches. We can only imagine how those Christians eagerly awaited his letters, and how they then shared them with others in the region. And how extraordinary it is that thousands of years later we are now hearing God's voice and learning more from the words Paul penned. Despite his captivity, his words were liberated by God to travel the world and through generations. It seems likely that even Paul could never have asked or imagined such a thing.

You might not be the apostle Paul, but even with your limitations and weaknesses God can elevate your gifts and use you to bless others in ways you could never imagine. It would be a tragedy if you disqualified yourself from being used by God because of... (fill in your own reason here – we all have them).

You may well feel inadequate or ill-equipped for what God has asked you to do. And if so, you are in excellent company, since most people we know and almost everybody we read about in the Bible felt the same way! The good news is, living a fruitful and faithful life is not about you and your brilliance – or your lack of it, anyway. We serve because we are empowered by God's Spirit, whose power is made perfect in our weakness (2 Corinthians 12:9). Our background, past mistakes, disappointments and all the experiences that make our story unique are known by God, and he delights in restoring us and raising people up from unexpected places in unexpected ways. And nothing in our life is wasted. In fact, as we minister to others and share our struggles as well as our strengths, we will often comfort others most where we have also been comforted (2 Corinthians 1:4). We will often help to bring freedom and hope where we have received the most freedom and hope.

This principle was reinforced again at Spring Harvest in 2023, when we invited a great guy called Dez Brown to speak one night. His full story is told in his book *Convicted or Condemned?*,[1] but in essence Dez was convicted and imprisoned after a fatal stabbing incident in East London. Dez shared his story with honesty and humility, and testified powerfully to the work of God in his life. In addition to becoming a minister, he went on to start a charity that works with vulnerable young people/adults and offenders, and he also advises on issues of race and justice. His story of redemption is remarkable, and it was a special night, not least because we were broadcasting live into prisons across the UK. The Holy Spirit was clearly at work as Dez spoke and in the time of ministry afterwards.

But as wonderful as that ministry was, it was what happened off the platform afterwards that was most remarkable. Dez began to make his way towards the resources area to meet people and to sign some books, and I (Cathy) was accompanying him. But before we'd gone very far, we were stopped by a lady who clearly wanted to speak to him. In a few moments this precious lady shared with him her experience of being abused by a gang member in London. It was clearly a significant moment for her. Dez listened intently and empathetically and said he was so sorry about her experience. She then responded by saying that she had forgiven the person involved, but could not hug him, so she wondered if she could possibly hug Dez in his place. Oh my. Well, Dez is a tall guy and she was a smaller woman, but he leaned down and kindly embraced that brave lady for a good long while as I stood back and watched Jesus at work. There was Dez, taking the place of her assailant, and there was Jesus, blessing and reassuring her and setting her free.

If ever I needed a reminder that God can redeem *anything* for his purposes, and that we should always pause for divine interruptions, that moment sufficed. With God's help not only can we rise above our past, but God will use every part of our story, even the parts we wish were different, to lift others up too.

What a God we serve.

Rise in grace and peace

The book of Ephesians ends as it begins, with the two words 'grace' and 'peace' being echoed, like a pair of brackets around the letter. Although the greeting at the start of Paul's letter is similar in format to a customary greeting at that time, with Paul no word choices are incidental. And so we read in 1:2, 'Grace and peace to you from God our Father and the Lord Jesus Christ.' And then, at the very end of the letter in 6:23–24, we read, 'Peace to the brothers and sisters, and love with faith from God the Father and the Lord Jesus Christ. Grace to all who love our Lord Jesus Christ with an undying love.'

These two words 'grace' and 'peace' are key words throughout Ephesians, so it is not surprising to see the letter bookended in this way. In 2:14 Jesus Christ is described as our peace, in 6:15 the good news is described as a gospel of peace, and God's people are to maintain unity of the Spirit through the bond of peace (4:3).

Similarly, we were saved by the immeasurable riches of his grace (2:5, 7–8), and the same grace has given to us gifts for service (4:7–13; 3:2, 7). As one commentator put it, 'If we want a concise summary of the good news which the whole letter announces, we could not find a better one than the three monosyllables "peace through grace"'.[2]

If peace is reconciliation with God and one another through Jesus, and grace is the reason and the means by which he did it,[3] then both are indispensable to us and to society.

Consider for a moment what peace and grace would look like where you live. How could your office, church or home be characterised by these two profoundly spiritual but very practical elements? Full disclosure: not every day in the Madavan home is calm, peaceful and grace-filled. We have had plenty of days of stress, frenetic activity and impatience. Nobody is perfect, after all! So how could we pursue more peace and grace? In a culture where being busy is considered a badge of honour, where stress has become a chronic condition, and ambition and influence are valuable commodities, is there a way of living that is more peace-filled? How might God want to recalibrate our stressed and striving souls again, to adjust our thinking, resting, relating and working in a way that gives glory to him?

Recently, author and pastor Pete Greig filmed an online video blog during a pilgrimage walk and quoted Bernard of Clairvaux, the twelfth-century abbot.[4] These ancient words seem as relevant today as they ever were:

Today there are many in the Church who act like canals, the reservoirs are far too rare... The canal simultaneously pours out what it receives; the reservoir retains the water till it is filled, then discharges the overflow without loss to itself. Learn to await this fullness before pouring out your gifts, do not try to be more generous than God.

To use Bernard of Clairvaux's analogy, we are often in such a rush spiritually, and in every other way, that we receive the refreshing shower of a sermon or a time of worship, perhaps, but it then flows straight back out as we serve, work and love, with our resources running dry almost immediately, until we slump, parched and tired, waiting for the next rainfall. What if we intentionally developed these spiritual reservoirs? What if we prioritised depth over breadth? What if, like Paul, our goal was to embrace peace and grace (and love and faith, which are also included in his closing words)? What if we yearned to grow in intimacy with God and maturity in Christ so that his love would overflow out of who we are? What if instead of a sprinkling of God's power and presence in our lives we were completely saturated with it?

What if?

These kinds of questions demand a response from us. And so does the letter to the Ephesians. If we want to be 'up and alive' in Jesus, and if we want to rise up and make a difference for him each day, we need to create space for the things of God and for fellowship with others. Prayer should be as high a priority in our lives as the new Netflix series, and giving to God should be as important as getting our next gadget or holiday. Perhaps, you might say, it would be impossible with your hectic schedule to create time for a day of prayer or a retreat. But would it? It might seem impossible to sign up for a course in theology, to serve regularly or to join a small group to increase your depth of knowledge and wisdom. But is it? We are all living in different circumstances, and for some of us it might even be hard to find time for a regular quiet time or even to read a book like this. Sometimes life is genuinely overwhelming, some seasons are more demanding than others and we do not all have the same capacity or flexibility. But while we need to be honest about what we *can't* do right now without guilt or shame, there are probably things we *can* do, and any time with Jesus is time well spent.

One thing is for sure: if we want to grow in maturity and unity as Paul consistently suggests, it doesn't happen overnight. No good relationship is built in a rush, and that is true when it comes to intimacy with God or anybody else. And God is not hurrying us or pressuring us, but instead he invites us to get to know him better. In his book *Three Mile an Hour God*, Japanese theologian Kosuke Koyama reminds us that Jesus came and *walked* with us. He was never hurried, and we can learn from the pace he chose.

> Love has its speed. It is a spiritual speed. It is a different kind of speed from the technological speed to which we are accustomed. It goes on in the depth of our life, whether we notice or not, at three miles an hour. It is the speed we walk and therefore the speed the love of God walks.[5]

It is interesting to consider that Jesus could have come at any time, including now, when he could have had a team creating YouTube videos and endless Insta reels. But he didn't. Even when he was here with his disciples, Jesus could have packed his schedule to the rafters, running from place to place. But he didn't. Jesus had time for fishing, praying and parties, and for weeping, storytelling, laughing and loving those around him. And yet he changed history. Perhaps, then, if we are moving too fast to pray, care, be hospitable, serve or listen well, we are simply moving too fast. It has been said that hurry and love are incompatible, like oil and water. If we want to learn to walk with Jesus, we need to do precisely that – *walk* with Jesus! And, wonderfully, Jesus would love to walk with us and accompany us through the highs and lows of each day.

Just as Paul's letter begins and ends with peace and grace, how good would it be if our comings and goings, our beginnings and endings, our mornings and evenings, were hallmarked with us learning to walk the Jesus way, with grace and peace? How good would it be if grace and peace increasingly characterised the way we worked, resolved conflict, served, shopped and lived in our communities? Even on days when we might not feel we have a lot to offer the world, we always have the grace and peace of Jesus – and that is more than enough. Because of God's grace and peace, we can be the ones who rise up and pray, lead, serve and love out of the overflow of God's reservoir of love in us.

Rise in faith

Paul was certainly a great man of faith, and a man whose faith resulted in him facing significant hardship and challenges. His faith also inspired the faith of others who knew him and who read his letters. Paul was so sure of the power and infinite love of God, his prayers were totally infused with that faith. No wonder his letters continue to build *our* faith today.

And, it must be said, we live in a time when faith is needed. Many of us, as individuals and churches, are still recalibrating in the wake of the Covid pandemic, whose effects will undoubtedly be felt for years. And yet there is also clearly an uprising of faith around us. It is as if we have woken up to the reality of life and death, and we have remembered how crucial our faith is and how fragile the Church can be. We have realised that our faith must be more than a Sunday thing, but many of us are also cherishing Sundays more than we did before we could no longer meet. With so much uncertainty around us, this is the time for us to rebuild our faith and to start stepping out in mission, compassion and making disciples again. The path might look unfamiliar at times, but we need to trust that God knows which way we should go.

A few years ago, we were fortunate enough to be able to have a short break in Morocco. While we were there, we decided to take a trip up the Atlas Mountains, the geological spine that separates the Sahara Desert on one side and the ocean on the other. In the Atlas Mountains we were to visit a village where the Berbers, or Amazigh people, live – as they have for thousands of years. We embarked upon our journey, rising mile after mile into the mountains, passing rivers, small settlements and breathtaking scenery, until we reached our destination. There, we were given a choice: we could settle by the river in a café (sensible – Mark's choice) or we could follow a Berber guide for a walk to a waterfall (Cathy's choice).

Have you ever signed up for something that was *far* harder than you expected? If you have, you will empathise when I (Cathy) tell you this was no tourist stroll as advertised. Instead, wearing my entirely unsuitable footwear, I followed our guide across rickety 'bridges', clambered over boulders, picked my way up narrow hillside paths and even jumped from rock to rock where necessary. Eventually we came to a wider river and our guide encouraged me to jump across it via a tiny rock in the middle. I looked at him as if he had lost his mind. Surely he had to be kidding! But no. I stood there, more than reluctant and less than confident.

'Come on,' he said. 'You can do it!'

I knew I definitely could not 'do it' and said that perhaps I should turn back or wait for the others to come back down again.

The guide looked at me again and said, 'Do you trust me?'

I replied, 'Sir, I have known you for about fifteen minutes, so actually no, not really!' A fair comment, I'm sure you'd agree.

He laughed and then explained to me that he had lived on this mountain his entire life. He had been raised on these narrow paths. There was not a stone, rock or bridge he did not know, and he could walk the trail with his eyes closed if necessary. He held out his hand for me to take and asked me again, 'Do you trust me?'

It's a big question, isn't it? Trust is normally earned, after all. Whose hand would we normally trust when we are in danger, unsure or need support? Who would we reach out for and who would we be less confident about? Who do we have faith in and who is more likely to let us down?

In this case, I chose to trust. I took hold of my guide's hand and, after helping me to quickly traverse the river, he set off at an alarming pace! The only thing I could physically do was watch his feet and step where he stepped, moment by moment, one move at a time. I didn't question him, I didn't second-guess his moves; in fact, I didn't have time to do anything other than fix my eyes on him and focus on the path ahead. After the river, we ascended a path together that I considered to be impossible – until it wasn't. And then, at the end, we were greeted by the most extraordinary waterfall and accompanying views that looked like something created by CGI. It was awe-inspiring.

Living by faith and following Jesus is essentially about trust. If we are able to step out courageously it is because we are confident in the One we are following. In fact, we will only ever be as courageous as we are confident in who is guiding us. When our Saviour, King, Friend and Good Shepherd asks us, 'Do you trust me?' it is because he knows the path ahead and has walked it before us. There is not a temptation, disappointment, rejection, fear or hope he has not experienced. He knows the difference that faith, grace, forgiveness and peace make. When we step out in obedience to him, maybe inviting somebody to an Alpha course or deciding to go on mission, he is with us and won't let us go. When we sign up to serve, share our faith, give generously, pray regularly or take on a role in our church or workplace that we feel is God's place for us, we need to focus on Jesus and follow closely. When we sense the nudge of the Holy Spirit calling us to cross over into new territory, to do things we never saw ourselves doing, we can advance because we do not go alone. We *could* not go alone! As it says in Hebrews, 'faith is confidence in what we hope for and assurance about what we do not see' (11:1), so we fix our eyes on Jesus, following him one step at a time, and what seemed invisible and improbable is suddenly possible.

So, do you trust him?

If everything we have read in Ephesians is true, it should alter how we think, see, live, love and trust Jesus. And our courage should grow as our confidence in him matures. So as we draw towards a close, we are reminded once more of the verse that has encapsulated and distilled so much of this letter in a few short words: 'I urge you to live a life worthy of the calling you have received' (4:1).

The *Message* version of these words adds a little extra colour to the heart of the original text: 'I want you to get out there and walk – better yet, run! – on the road God called you to travel. I don't want any of you sitting around on your hands. I don't want anyone strolling off, down some path that goes nowhere' (4:1–2).

Be encouraged – you have indeed received a calling, and you have been called by name by the One who knows and loves you. This truth is crystal clear in Paul's writing. Again, you are called. You have a purpose. You are not a mistake, and you are supposed to be here at this time in history. You have been forgiven and redeemed and repositioned eternally by a God who has called you to share his love today. God has a unique path he has called only you to travel.

When I (Mark) was called to be a minister it was a public affirmation of what God had already affirmed in me. But it is not just ministers, worship leaders and preachers who are called. Paul writes to all of God's holy people (1:1). It is wonderful when the body of Christ acknowledges and affirms the gifts and anointing of those in every area of church life, be that administration, graphic design, working with children or hospitality, for example. It is inspiring when the church anoints and releases people to serve on mission, in our communities or in the workplace. We are all called, whoever we are, and wherever our front line may be.[6]

Whatever your background, age, education, race, gender, ability or social status, you are called to rise in faith. A pastor is not more called than an electrician; a doctor is not more called than an administrator. We are called because of our position in Christ, not our position in the Church or the world. While the media might elevate the billionaires and the supermodels, and our culture might define success by our income or our social media reach, our faith is what unites us and sets us apart for whatever God asks us to do.

And as we walk purposefully in our calling, by faith, we not only rise up ourselves, but we lift others up too. As Jesus reaches out to us, we too hold out our hand to others and show them that with support they can cross terrain they never thought was possible. As parents, colleagues, friends and neighbours, we are called to show the hope of Jesus, who helps us all to rise up and make a difference. We should particularly hold out a hand to the rising generations of children and young people who need mothers and fathers and aunties and uncles in the faith, to hold them as they navigate the turbulent terrain of our culture. Together, we can embark on new adventures of faith, going far beyond what we thought was possible, growing in depth together but also in faith for what God might do in this day in our nation.

Finally, in essence Paul urges us to become more of who we already are in Christ. As John Stott summarises it: 'The whole letter is thus a magnificent combination of Christian doctrine and Christian duty, Christian faith and Christian life, what God has done through Christ and what we must be and do in consequence.'[7]

In other words, if we understand who we are, we will gladly live accordingly. We are called and chosen as adopted children of God, so we should be secure in it and live a life worthy of it. We are transformed, living in the kingdom of light rather than the kingdom of darkness, so we should behave like it. We have been given a new community and a new relationship with God, so our character and our unity should reflect it. As we gratefully receive and own what we have been given, we will stand firm against compromise, and we will not be tempted to walk down paths that lead us back to where we came from. We have been given so much – every spiritual blessing! Our lives should be a response of worship and thanks to Jesus for all he has gained for us. We are not just here to observe others or make do with a wishy-washy faith. Paul urges us to know who we are and to live therefore for Jesus, even if it is costly.

We are his people and we are 'up and alive'. We have been called for a purpose to rise up in his power, to know him and make a difference, for his name's sake. We are called to rise and radiate God's holy life of peace, grace, unity, reconciliation and righteousness.

This is glorious living indeed!

So, friends:

Look up and give thanks for every spiritual blessing you have received .
Wake up and embrace the new life you are now living.
Dress up in the spiritual outfits that are fitting for the new you.
Stand up together on the ground that has already been won for you.
Rise up in the grace, peace and faith that God has deposited in you for a purpose.

Or, in other words:

Live a life worthy of the calling you have received.

Rise up – working it out

Reflect

Can you name three people who you would say have risen above their circumstances to give glory to God despite their challenges?

What would it mean for God to use you and your story to bring freedom or comfort to others where you have needed it yourself? Pray or journal about this.

Recalibrate

- How hurried, busy or stressed are you most of the time? What would an increased measure of grace and peace look like
  - in your home;
  - in your workplace;
  - in your church;
  - in your neighbourhood?

- How could you be a grace- and peace-bringer in these places?

- If God reached out his hand today and asked you, 'Do you trust me?', where might he be leading you? What new faith adventures or steps of faith is he asking you to consider?

Rejoice

Risen Lord Jesus, Prince of peace, Giver of grace,

Thank you that I do not walk alone but with you today. I take a moment to fully receive and appreciate your faithfulness and all you have given to me. Help me to rise above my circumstances and trust you fully. I pray I would rise up in faith, hope and love, and lift others towards you too. And I thank you that I will rise again with you for eternity. Holy Spirit, fill me afresh today so that I might live a life worthy of the calling I have received.

For you and your glory. Amen.

A note of thanks

We have both been so privileged to write this book for SPCK and Spring Harvest, where it will help to shape the theme of the 2024 event. We would prefer not to count the years we have been involved with Spring Harvest as we wish to kid ourselves that we are younger than we are, but we remain deeply grateful for this incredible ministry and the friendships we have formed as a result.

We particularly wish to thank Abby Guinness and Lisa Olsworth-Peter, whose leadership of the Spring Harvest event is exemplary by any standards, and also the Spring Harvest Planning Group (wonderfully led by the Revd Cris Rogers) who, apart from being superb and supportive friends, serve and pray so faithfully to see the Church in the UK and beyond strengthened and encouraged. Thanks also to Malcolm Duncan, whose feedback and theological reflection have been, as ever, hugely helpful. Thank you to Phil Loose and the entire team who work behind the scenes to bless the thousands of people who come to the Spring Harvest festival and then resource them throughout the year.

Thank you also to the team at SPCK. We are so thankful for your hard work in bringing this book into the world. It really is a team effort, and we sincerely appreciate you.

Thank you (as always) to our wonderful daughters, Naomi and Izzy, and to our many friends who have prayed and listened to us panic about deadlines. We couldn't do it without your support.

But mostly, we do thank God for the faith journey he has taken us on over many years. His presence and his word have been our companion, guide, inspiration, strength and place of refuge. It has been an honour to write this book and to study Ephesians more deeply. We hope and pray it will bring Paul's magnificent letter to the Ephesians to life in new ways for every reader. It has genuinely been a privilege to spend this time together with you in Paul's words. We pray it will bless you as it has blessed us.

Here's to being 'up and alive' in Jesus!

Notes

Introduction

1 Hawthorne, G. F., Martin, R. P. and Reid, D. G. (eds), *Dictionary of Paul and His Letters* (Downers Grove, IL: InterVarsity Press, 2005), p. 249.

2 Hawthorne, Martin and Reid, *Dictionary of Paul and His Letters*, p. 250.

3 Antipater, *Greek Anthology*, IX.58, public domain.

4 Hawthorne, Martin and Reid, *Dictionary of Paul and His Letters*, p. 250.

5 Acts 19 tells of people burning their sorcery scrolls, and silversmiths rioting against Paul.

6 Scholars debate not only the authorship of Ephesians but also whether the letter was written to this one church or a wider selection of churches in the area. We will work on the assumption that the Ephesians were at least among the recipients, and that Paul was responsible for the content in some form.

7 Lincoln, A. T., *Ephesians*, Word Biblical Commentary, Vol. 42 (Waco, TX: Word Books, 2005), p. xlviii.

8 Wright, T., *Paul for Everyone: The prison letters* (London: SPCK, 2014), p. 3.

9 We would highly recommend, for starters, Wright, T., *Paul for Everyone: The prison letters*.

10 Stott, J. R. W., *The Message of Ephesians: God's new society*, 2nd edn (with study guide), The Bible Speaks Today (Leicester: Inter-Varsity Press, 1991), p. 15.

1 Look up

1 Lincoln, A. T., *Ephesians*, Word Biblical Commentary, Vol. 42 (Waco, TX: Word Books, 2005), p. 11.

2 Retinitis pigmentosa is the condition Mark has inherited, for those of

you who are interested in learning more. Mark was diagnosed in his mid-twenties and has very little sight remaining now.

3 James 1:2–4, for example, alongside the wider experiences of many biblical writers or characters who did not have an easy life by any benchmark. That's not to say we don't make mistakes or that we can't grow in maturity, but many hardships we face are not of our making.

4 Stott, J. R. W., *The Message of Ephesians: God's new society*, 2nd edn (with study guide), The Bible Speaks Today (Leicester: Inter-Varsity Press, 1991), p. 35.

5 Stott, *The Message of Ephesians*, p. 36.

6 The truths in this passage remind us why the adoption of children is still such a significant way of showing God's love and care. We would commend the charity www.homeforgood.org.uk as a helpful resource and support for those seeking to show God's love in such a significant way.

7 Wright, T., *Paul for Everyone: The prison letters* (London: SPCK, 2014), p. 9.

8 Wright, *Paul for Everyone*, p. 9.

9 Stott, *The Message of Ephesians*, p. 34.

10 Stott, *The Message of Ephesians*, p. 34.

11 Barclay, W., *The Daily Study Bible: The Letters to the Galatians and Ephesians* (Edinburgh: St Andrew Press, 1976), 81.

12 Wright, *Paul for Everyone*, p. 9.

13 Wright, *Paul for Everyone*, p. 9.

14 Spiritual disciplines might include prayer, fasting, fellowship, simplicity, solitude, generosity, study and journalling. We would highly recommend John Mark Comer's teaching on spiritual disciplines – check out www.practicingtheway.org for more.

15 We would recommend the teaching and books of Dr Tania Harris, whose research on how individuals and churches hear and discern God's voice is fascinating and invaluable. See: www.godconversations.com.

16 Ephesians 1:10. This is God's ultimate fulfilled purpose and plan – a glorious and complete togetherness where everything in creation and God's people will be unified in and under Christ for eternity.

17 Stott, *The Message of Ephesians*, p. 49.

18 This is a major theme in Cathy's book *Why Less Means More: Making space for what matters most* (London: SPCK, 2023).

2 Wake up

1 Not only in the letter to the Ephesians. Here and elsewhere the theme of death and life is fundamental.

2 Barclay, W., *The Daily Study Bible: The Letters to the Galatians and Ephesians* (Edinburgh: St Andrew Press, 1976), p. 95.

3 Barclay, *Daily Study Bible*, p. 96.

4 Stott, J. R. W., *The Message of Ephesians: God's new society*, 2nd edn (with study guide), The Bible Speaks Today (Leicester: Inter-Varsity Press, 1991), p. 71.

5 Stott, *The Message of Ephesians*, p. 69.

6 Stott, *The Message of Ephesians*, p. 72.

7 Available at: https://www.cru.org/us/en/train-and-grow/share-the-gospel/the-gospel-in-all-its-forms.html (accessed 3 November 2023).

8 While in James 2:18 it seems to suggest that our faith is evidenced by our works, in fact this is not a contradiction of Paul, as some have suggested. James's words suggest that our faith is not held in a vacuum – our beliefs and behaviour are linked, and our life should indeed reveal and demonstrate our faith.

9 Peterson, E., *A Long Obedience in the Same Direction: Discipleship in an instant society* (Westmont, IL: Inter-Varsity Press, 2000).

10 The Beatitudes (Matthew 5) are part of Jesus' famous Sermon on the Mount. Malcolm Duncan's book *Flipped – Life in the upside-down kingdom* (London: SPCK, 2023), written for Spring Harvest 2023, is a superb exploration of this vital theme.

11 Full disclosure: this was almost certainly written or said by David Kinnaman from Barna Labs, but the source seems impossible to find! We will give him the credit anyway. It's the sort of brilliant thing he would say.

12 This article by Tim Keller says a lot more about some forms of the gospel in greater depth: https://www.cru.org/us/en/train-and-grow/

share-the-gospel/the-gospel-in-all-its-forms.html (accessed 3 November 2023).

13 *Useful places to go for further advice*: For church or charity issues on safeguarding or concerns about culture: https://thirtyoneeight.org/ and for those who wish to learn more about or who are affected by domestic abuse or controlling relationships: https://www.restored-uk.org.

14 For further reading and an excellent assessment tool and resources to help you and your church to explore discipleship and spiritual formation: https://www.wearemakingdisciples.com.

15 Visit: https://alpha.org.uk for more information on Alpha.

16 By no means an exhaustive list.

17 Available at: https://pastorrick.com/your-shape-shows-your-purpose (accessed 4 November 2023).

3 Dress up

1 Or 'the flesh', as the Bible sometimes calls it.

2 We understand that the consumption of food is not as simple as this for some people. For those with eating issues – restricted or emotional eating, for example – choices are more complicated. Our use of this metaphor is simply to explain that there are external and internal battles we all have to fight.

3 Stott, J. R. W., *The Message of Ephesians: God's new society*, 2nd edn (with study guide), The Bible Speaks Today (Leicester: Inter-Varsity Press, 1991), p. 180.

4 Lincoln, A. T., *Ephesians*, Word Biblical Commentary, Vol. 42 (Waco, TX: Word Books, 2005), p. 278.

5 Stott, *The Message of Ephesians*, p. 188.

6 Stott, *The Message of Ephesians*, pp. 262–63.

7 Shirer, P., *The Armor of God* (Nashville, TN: LifeWay Press, 2022), p. 16.

8 See thoughts from Richard Rohr at: https://cac.org/daily-meditations/principalities-and-powers-2023-05-15 (accessed 7 November 2023).

9 See Shirer, *The Armor of God*, p. 20.

10 Insight included from Stott, *The Message of Ephesians*.

11 Shirer, *The Armor of God*, p. 35.
12 Barclay, W., *The Daily Study Bible: The Letters to the Galatians and Ephesians* (Edinburgh: St Andrew Press, 1976), p. 184.
13 Again, we recommend Cathy's book *Why Less Means More: Making space for what matters most* (London: SPCK, 2023). Each chapter helps you to recalibrate and create margin where you need it most. John Mark Comer's book *The Ruthless Elimination of Hurry* (London: Hodder & Stoughton, 2019) is also excellent.
14 Greig, P., *How to Pray: A simple guide for normal people* (London: Hodder & Stoughton, 2019).
15 Highly recommended is the free Lectio365 app from 24-7 Prayer, which embraces this PRAY habit and rhythm of prayer and Scripture each day. It can be read or listened to.

4 Stand up

1 We are aware that for many in the disabled community, the phrase 'stand up' is potentially problematic. Some people cannot physically stand up or stand firm for any length of time and we appreciate that. Primarily, this is a metaphorical statement of intent, and we know how courageous and committed many in the disabled community are about standing up for themselves, for others and for Jesus.
2 Peter Scazzero's books about emotional healthiness very helpfully and thoroughly address the issues of our shadow side.
3 Romans 12:2 says, 'Do not conform to the pattern of this world, but be transformed by the renewing of your mind.' Modern science shows us that neuroplasticity 'is the ability of neural networks in the brain to change through growth and reorganization' (see: https://en.wikipedia.org/wiki/Neuroplasticity). Cognitive behavioural therapy (CBT) examines how your thoughts affect your behaviour and 'focuses on how your thoughts, beliefs and attitudes affect your feelings and actions' (see: https://www.mind.org.uk/information-support/drugs-and-treatments/talking-therapy-and-counselling/cognitive-behavioural-therapy-cbt/#WhatIsCBT).
4 Apart from getting professional or medical help where necessary, we would recommend organisations like Kintsugi Hope (https://

kintsugihope.com), Sanctuary Mental Health Ministries (https://
sanctuarymentalhealth.org/uk) and the Mind and Soul Foundation
(https://www.mindandsoulfoundation.org) for more information
about healthy thinking and emotional well-being.

5 For those who struggle with addiction to alcohol or other substances,
specialist support is needed. Alcoholics Anonymous and Narcotics
Anonymous provide superb help and support. For many people, the
choice to stand firm in the face of addiction is incredibly difficult and
courageous.

6 *The Imitation of Christ* by Thomas à Kempis is freely available online
in the public domain and in numerous printed editions.

7 See also Galatians 3:28, which says, 'There is neither Jew nor Gentile,
neither slave nor free, nor is there male and female, for you are all
one in Christ Jesus.'

8 Stott, J. R. W., *The Message of Ephesians: God's new society*, 2nd edn
(with study guide), The Bible Speaks Today (Leicester: Inter-Varsity
Press, 1991), p. 219.

9 Stott, *The Message of Ephesians*, p. 219.

10 There are many excellent books, commentaries and articles that more
fully explore the issues here. One helpful resource is Marg Mowczko's
website for insight into Ephesians 5 from an egalitarian perspective,
including numerous articles on Ephesians 5, available at: https://
margmowczko.com/?s=ephesians+5 (accessed 10 November 2023).

11 Barclay, W., *The Daily Study Bible. The Letters to the Galatians and
Ephesians* (Edinburgh: St Andrew Press, 1976), p. 175.

12 We would highly recommend resources, events and courses from
Care for the Family for all parents.

13 Wright, T., *Paul for Everyone: The prison letters* (London: SPCK,
2014), p. 70.

5 Rise up

1 Brown, D. and Saunders, M., *Convicted or Condemned?* (Milton
Keynes: Authentic, 2005). Dez is the founder of the charity
Spark2Life, see: https://spark2life.co.uk.

2 Stott, J. R. W., *The Message of Ephesians: God's new society*, 2nd edn

(with study guide), The Bible Speaks Today (Leicester: Inter-Varsity Press, 1991), p. 28.

3 Stott, *The Message of Ephesians*, p. 291.

4 A video podcast of Pete Greig's pilgrimage from Iona to Lindisfarne, Day 9, available at: https://www.youtube.com/watch?v=JMEg2kfRkN0 (accessed 22 November 2023).

5 Kosuke Koyama, *Three Mile an Hour God* (London: SCM Press, 2021), pp. 6–7.

6 London Institute for Contemporary Christianity (LICC) continues to do a marvellous job of equipping people for living out their faith as disciples of Jesus on every front line, in the workplace, in schools, in homes or churches. See: https://licc.org.uk.

7 Stott, *The Message of Ephesians*, p. 25.